INTEGRATING SCHOOL AND FAMILY COUNSELING: PRACTICAL SOLUTIONS

Edited by
Lynn D. Miller

THE FAMILY PSYCHOLOGY AND COUNSELING SERIES

AMERICAN
COUNSELING
ASSOCIATION

Developed Collaboratively by the American Counseling Association and
the International Association of Marriage and Family Counselors

INTEGRATING SCHOOL AND FAMILY COUNSELING: PRACTICAL SOLUTIONS

10 9 8 7 6 5 4 3 2 1

American Counseling Association
5999 Stevenson Avenue
Alexandria, VA 22304

Director of Publications
Carolyn C. Baker

Production Manager
Bonny E. Gaston

Copy Editor
Cheryl Duksta

Cover design by Martha Woolsey

LB
1027.5
.I57
2002

Library of Congress Cataloging-in-Publication Data

Integrating school and family counseling: practical solutions / by Lynn D. Miller [editor].
　　p. cm.
Includes bibliographical references.
ISBN 1-55620-184-2 (alk. paper)
　　1. Educational counseling. 2. Home and school. I. Miller, Lynn D. II. American Counseling Association.

LB1027.5. I57 2002
371.7'13—dc21

2002016402

The Family Psychology and Counseling Series

Counseling African American Families
Jo-Ann Lipford Sanders, PhD, and Carla Bradley, PhD

Counseling the Aging and Their Families
Irene Deitch, PhD, and Candace Ward Howell, MS

Counseling Asian Families From a Systems Perspective
Kit S. Ng, PhD

Counseling Families With Chronic Illness
Susan McDaniel, PhD

Ethical Casebook for the Practice of Marriage and Family Counseling
Patricia Stevens, PhD

Feminist Family Therapy
Kathleen M. May, PhD

High-Performing Families: Causes, Consequences, and Clinical Solutions
Bryan E. Robinson, PhD, and Nancy D. Chase, PhD

Integrating School and Family Counseling: Practical Solutions
Lynn D. Miller, PhD

Integrative and Biopsychosocial Therapy: Maximizing Treatment Outcomes With Individuals and Couples
Len Sperry, MD, PhD

Mid-Life Divorce Counseling
Lita Linzer Schwartz, PhD

Social Construction in Couple and Family Counseling
John D. West, EdD, Donald L. Bubenzer, PhD, and James Robert Bitter, EdD

Techniques in Marriage and Family Counseling, Volume One
Richard E. Watts, PhD

Techniques in Marriage and Family Counseling, Volume Two
Richard E. Watts, PhD

Transitioning From Individual to Family Counseling
Charles Huber, PhD

Understanding Stepfamilies: Implications for Assessment and Treatment
Debra Huntley, PhD

Advisory Board

■■■
THE FAMILY PSYCHOLOGY AND COUNSELING SERIES

Table of Contents

PART III. OUTCOME RESEARCH IMPLICATIONS

From the Series Editor

Children benefit when schools and families work together. This is not a new idea, and most professionals—in theory—endorse this type of collaboration. The reason collaboration continues to be a newsworthy topic is that it seldom happens in our schools today. Schools and families continue to single out individual children as having problems and treat the children independent of their families, in isolation.

Lynn Miller and her colleagues have created a compact and efficient volume that provides the skills and techniques that can put theory into everyday practice. This book provides a rationale and the research support for working with families from a school base. It also provides specific techniques for using solution-focused tools, conducting family therapy with children, working with parents and teachers, and working with individuals from a family perspective.

I have worked for more than 30 years as a school counselor and have found these ideas and strategies to really make a difference. They create the type of change that is supported by research and results in observable and apparent behaviors. Reading this volume will convince you that we can no longer isolate and treat children without treating the context in which they live. Using the ideas in this book will help you create a healthier community.

—Jon Carlson, PsyD, EdD
Series Editor

From the Series Editor

Preface

This book is an attempt to formalize what many school counselors have struggled with for decades: Working with a troubled child in a school setting is far more effective if the counselor can also work with the child's family. This is wishful thinking, more often than not, because school counselors have been sidetracked by a myriad of duties other than preventive, developmentally appropriate services to students. The reasons for this vary. The counselor: student ratio, although suggested ideally to be 250:1 by the American School Counselor Association, burgeons in some schools at 800:1 or more. Other tasks, often administrative, also interfere with providing direct services: course scheduling, credit counting, meetings, covering absent teachers' classes, and other administrative details.

School counselors may feel a deficit in their graduate training in relation to being able to respond comfortably to the prospect of working with a child's family. Although many school counselors are trained in consultation theory and collaboration techniques to use with teachers, staff, outside community resource people, and families, these techniques are often not sufficient. As prevention specialists, counselors are trained to refer troubled children and their families to outside therapy specialists. However, many families cannot afford outside specialists or feel reluctant to seek help outside of the school. The stigma of mental disorder remains strong and perhaps has even greater strength when a family considers a child possibly getting a lifelong label.

To complicate matters, family therapists in private practice often feel ill equipped to work with children. This may reflect a deficit in their training or a greater comfort level with the higher cognitive ability of adults to express themselves or perhaps indicate a belief that improving the marital relationship will improve the family environment.

Therefore, getting children and their families appropriate help is a circular dilemma; school counselors want to see children in a counseling setting with the support of their families but refer these families out because of time, perhaps training, and role definition restraints. Family counselors feel awkward including children in sessions and often do not because of a different focus, perhaps training limitations, and their own psychological barriers.

In this book, we offer practical suggestions for school counselors to begin integrating family counseling methods into their practice. All seven authors have been practicing or researching school counselors at the elementary, middle, and secondary levels. This book is unique in that it is written for school counselors by veteran school counselors. In chapter 1, the author provides a brief overview of the classic variations in family systems theory. Research is reported that supports school counselors' suspicions that children perform better in schools when they have the support of their families. A counseling model is also presented. William Nicoll, in chapter 2, continues the discussion on the need to incorporate family counseling in school settings, focusing on parenting style. In chapter 3, Bobbie Birdsall presents a solution-focused approach for school counselors to adopt in their settings because this approach is effective, time efficient, and powerful. Chapter 4 is a compendium of ideas and suggestions for concrete interventions to use when working with children and their families in school settings and is written by Alan Carr.

Chapter 5 focuses on encouraging and including parents and teachers using systems theory for improving the academic success of children. Deanna Hawes details practical suggestions for school counselors to use that appeal to the coordinating and collaborative skills of school counselors. Chapter 6 suggests ways of working with the family when the family refuses to come to counseling at the school. This approach uses the concepts of systems thinking with the individual child. The final chapter, by Sue Whiston and Carla Teed, is an overview of the research examining school counseling activities. The authors strongly encourage school counselors to be informed about evidenced-based programs and to seek further training in family therapy approaches that have been endorsed by the

Centers for Disease Control and Prevention and the U.S. surgeon general.

It is our hope that school counselors, in this age of school reform, become strong advocates for their schools and profession by including family counseling training, rigorous research, and integration of systems theory in their careers.

—Lynn D. Miller, PhD

Biographies

Lynn D. Miller, PhD, is a sessional instructor in the counseling psychology department at the University of British Columbia. She started her career as a classroom teacher at the secondary level and then went on to be a school counselor at the elementary and secondary levels. Following this, she earned her PhD, with an emphasis in integrating mental health services for children and families, at the University of Colorado, where she worked for approximately 8 years before moving to Canada. She is registered as a psychologist and has a small private practice. Dr. Miller has long been interested in helping children be more successful in school settings. She believes that the family is critical to academic success, and she focuses her research on the search for ways to deliver mental health programs to families in school settings. She is currently the president of the Anxiety Disorders Association of British Columbia (2000–2002).

Jon Carlson, PsyD, EdD, is distinguished professor at Governors State University in University Park, Illinois, and the director of the Lake Geneva Wellness Clinic in Wisconsin. He is the editor of *The Family Journal: Counseling and Therapy for Couples and Families* and has served as president of the International Association of Marriage and Family Counselors. Dr. Carlson holds a diplomate in family psychology from the American Board of Professional Psychology. He is a fellow of the American Psychological Association and a certified sex therapist by the American Association of

Sex Educators, Counselors, and Therapists. He has authored more than 25 books and 125 professional articles. He has received numerous awards for his professional contributions from major professional organizations, including the American Counseling Association, the Association for Counselor Education and Supervision, and the American Psychological Association. Dr. Carlson and his spouse, Laura, are the parents of five children and grandparents of two.

Contributors

Bobbie Birdsall, PhD, is an associate professor in the Counselor Education Department at Boise State University, Boise, Idaho.

Alan Carr, PhD, is the director of the Doctoral Training Programme in Clinical Psychology at University College Dublin and a consultant at the Clanwilliam Institute for Marital and Family Therapy in Dublin.

The late *Deanna Hawes*, PhD, was an associate professor in the Counselor Education and Rehabilitation Department at Emporia State University, Lawrence, Kansas.

William G. Nicoll, PhD, is a professor and department chair in the Department of Counselor Education at Florida Atlantic University, Boca Raton, Florida.

Carla M. Teed, MA, is a student in the Department of Counseling and Educational Psychology at Indiana University.

Susan C. Whiston, PhD, is a professor in the Department of Counseling and Educational Psychology at Indiana University.

PART

INTRODUCTION TO FAMILY SYSTEMS THEORY

1

Overview of Family Systems Counseling in a School Setting

Lynn D. Miller, PhD

Children ages 5 to 18 spend nearly half of their waking hours from September until early June either in school or getting ready for school. School is, indeed, one of the main focal points in a child's life—the other being the child's home. These two environments are inextricably linked and have a significant influence on each other. Schools traditionally, however, have had limited forays into a child's home life, and conversely, families leave the education of their children largely to the schools. School counselors have long suspected that when a child has difficulty in a school setting, the confluence of these two systems—the family and the school—provides more information, greater perspective, and typically mutually beneficial support for the child. Educators, concerned with the development of the whole child, have in large part understood that the mental health of a child is as critical to the child's healthy development and growth as reading, writing, and arithmetic (Harter, 1993). To ensure this mental health, the two systems must integrate to a greater degree when a child's behavior or emotional stability jeopardizes success in the academic arena. One way to facilitate this integration is to offer family counseling in the school setting.

Overview of Family Systems Theory

Family systems counseling informally started in the early 20th century, when Alfred Adler began forming parent groups. Adler believed that people are born good and as social beings are motivated by two broad goals: social responsibility and the power to control enough of their own lives to make conscious decisions. The original social group, the family, provides the foundation for and contributes much toward the development of our understanding of social relationships. He emphasized a positive, developmental view of human nature that parallels much of the educational structure in schools. These parent groups eventually developed into what we recognize today as family therapy.

Family counseling, or family therapy, can take many forms and often reflects either the counselor's perspective and training (i.e., a systems perspective rather than an individual counseling perspective) or the composition of people attending the counseling session. Family counseling can involve an individual, a couple, a parent, a child or children, members of an extended family or unrelated people living in the same home, or the entire family, nuclear or intergenerational.

The key difference between individual counseling and family counseling is that in family counseling the focus is on the family and its members' interactions and relationships. An individual's maladaptive (i.e., dysfunctional) behavior is therefore seen as a manifestation of dysfunction within the system or, at a minimum, as affecting the system negatively. For example, a child's consistent aggressive playground behavior is seen not exclusively as the individual child's lack of impulse control but in the larger context of a family system characterized perhaps as chaotic or occasionally violent. Systems counseling looks at circular influences (i.e., the idea that events are related through a series of interactions and feedback loops, for example, "I discipline you because you are rebellious," "No, I rebel because you discipline me"), rather than focusing on more linear influences (e.g., parents fight one night, which adversely effects the child's sleep in the home, which then influences the child's school performance the next day) as an individual counselor might do. One key feature of circular causality is not to find blame (after all, where does a circle begin or end?) but to get away from blame and to find more successful ways of interacting.

Family therapy approaches, many associated with distinct techniques or interventions, have proliferated. Classic family approaches reviewed in this chapter include multigenerational, humanistic, structural, strategic, and postmodern. In looking at the differences of each approach and thinking about the charismatic leaders who first developed them, one theme remains constant: Family counseling is fundamentally about changing the entire family. When change happens for the individual in a family context, all members of the system are affected. These theoretical approaches are translated into practical applications throughout the chapter. In addition, basic questions of why family counseling is important both for children and parents are answered, evidence of effectiveness of family interventions at school sites is presented, a five-step counseling model is offered, benefits and pitfalls of such a model are examined, and the question of counselor preparation and training is discussed.

Summaries of Family Counseling Approaches

Multigenerational Approach

The multigenerational approach, also known as the family of origin or transgenerational approach, headed by Murray Bowen, James Framo, and others, stresses exploring family of origin patterns and includes investigation into behaviors from three generations. For instance, a multigenerational approach toward school failure might search for academic patterns in school success or education values in the parents and grandparents. Often we are influenced by our parents' values, without questioning if those values are important for us. This is commonly seen in career selection ("Grandpa was a hardworking union man, I am a hardworking union man, and you need to be looking at what a union job can offer you!"). These emotional legacies both focus and narrow our options. The keys to change are discovering how values are transmitted, using a cognitive process of questioning family issues, and encouraging differentiation.

Human Validation and Experiential Approaches (Humanistic Approach)

Virginia Satir was a warm, charming, and loving therapist who taught family members how to communicate openly. She demonstrated unspoken issues and feelings by using family sculpture and drama techniques. She and Carl Whitaker, an experiential therapist, were active and spontaneous participants in family counseling, often touching and engaging the family in physical demonstrations. High use of empathy and self-disclosure is thought to model positive communication and encourage self-esteem. In a school setting, caution is always urged in physical demonstrations of support for students. Human validation should be expressed more as unconditional positive regard, self-esteem enhancing activities, and unqualified respect for others.

Structural Approach

Developed largely by Salvador Minuchin, the structural approach focuses on boundaries and the hierarchical nature of families. A healthy family requires an executive subsystem (spousal, couple, or adult), which accommodates each person's uniqueness. When this autonomous system operates in a leadership position, a healthy environment evolves: Security, rules, consequences, and support for the sibling subsystem are clearly developed. Problems occur when these subsystems cross into each other's territories, that is, when parents reject responsibility in favor of less-mature and childish roles, and when children take on too much responsibility for adult chores, tasks, or roles. School counselors often understand when young children are placed in parenting roles (e.g., the older sister baby-sitting and caring for a number of younger siblings) so frequently that they cannot endure the stress of the responsibility. A structuralist seeks to reestablish the appropriate responsibilities of the child and reassign these duties to the hierarchical categories of the parent subsystem.

Strategic Approach

People often solve problems with the same approach, even when the approach is unsuccessful and the problem continues. For instance, parents often engage in combative arguments with adolescents about homework completion. Even though there may not be an increase in time on task in homework or success in handing in homework, parents continue to yell at and badger their children to do homework. Badgering, nagging, and reminding are logical strategies many people use to motivate others. Strategic practitioners believe families operate logically or functionally to maintain homeostatic balance in the family. This approach, authored by Jay Haley, Cloe Madanes, and Milton Erickson, focuses on the "stuck" interactional sequences in a family. A strategic counselor is problem focused and prescriptive ("You need to establish a consistently arranged homework hour that is supervised by the parent and takes place irrefutably every night and the consequence of not showing up is . . . "), and the intervention can often be paradoxical.

Social Constructionism

Social constructionism is also known as postmodernism and can include narrative, feminist, brief, and integrative approaches. Social constructivists function collaboratively with a family and believe that people are shaped by interactions with others and therefore have no one constant "core" self. Because people experience events differently, there is no one true explanation of any event. Social constructionism focuses on the future and how best to solve problems, rather than on understanding the cause of problems. Tom Anderson, Harlene Anderson, Harold Goolishian, Michael White, David Epston, William O'Hanlon, Michelle Weiner-Davis, Steve de Shazer, and Insoo Kim Berg, and many feminist family therapists (e.g., Carol Anderson, Monica McGoldrick, Peggy Papp, Marianne Walters, and Rachel Hare-Mustin), have all shaped this movement with ideas that often counter the basic tenets of systems thinking: Perhaps people do not play equal parts in family dynamics and do not share equally in power and responsibility. A social constructivist listens carefully, adopts a position of "not knowing," challenges stereotypes, and supports each person's position in the family. Stories of each person's experience are elicited, and these life stories are reauthored with a new solution or newly constructed life story.

Family Counseling: Including Children

In the family therapy field, little agreement exists about how, if, and when to involve children in family sessions in private practice settings (Stith, Rosen, McCollum, & Herman, 1996).Family therapy often ignores children altogether, focuses on the adult couple relationship, and has been accused of "not seeing the children at all" (Diller, 1991, p. 23). In a recent large study of licensed marriage and family practitioners, participants claimed families formed only 12% of their caseload: The remaining caseload consisted of 49% individuals, 23% couples, and 15% combination (Doherty & Simmons, 1996). This may be a reflection of the presenting problem being more appropriate for the adults (i.e., an extramarital affair), or it may be a reflection of the counselor feeling more competent in dealing with issues that trouble adults. A clear implication, however, is that today's problems are increasingly manifested by today's youth, and the family is a critical component in prevention and intervention in childhood and adolescent problems. It is a professional, if not moral, obligation for the school counselor to involve the adult family members in counseling, especially if private family practitioners are ambivalent about involving children in sessions.

Why Family Counseling Is Important for Both Schoolchildren and Parents

"Counseling and education for parents and their children can alleviate stress, improve self-concept, and reduce social/behavioral problems" (Kale & Landreth, 1999). Parenting is stressful. Parents experience predictable developmental tasks of childhood and simultaneously negotiate family life-cycle benchmarks, typically with no training other than the modeling provided by their own parents. Some parents consult self-help books. Fewer take parenting classes. Many talk to friends or neighbors with similarly aged children. However, many of these developmental experiences provide circumstances and situations that are constantly changing and do not conform to any one set of rules.

When a child experiences more difficulties than other children, the parenting tasks and stressors are exacerbated. Gerald Patterson, a leading authority of parent training and childhood emotional and behavioral disturbance, has claimed that conduct problems "in children and adolescents [are] a behavioral problem, not a mental health problem. The causes lie in the social environment, not in the minds of the youngsters" (Forgatch & Patterson, 1998, p. 85). Although many parents shake their heads in confusion about their child and ask, "What in the world is wrong with this kid?" perhaps the more logical question should be "What in the world is affecting my child so profoundly so that he or she is acting this way?" The child is often reacting to the environment and—inadvertently or unknowingly—bearing or manifesting the symptom of this stress or dysfunction for the family. As the child's behavior escalates, the circular nature of family systems theory can be easily seen: The family in turn experiences the stress of the child's increasingly problematic behavior. This spiraling negative energy continues to fuel both the child's response and the family's stress until something dramatic happens.

Are Childhood Behavior Problems Getting Worse?

Achenbach and Howell in 1993 published one of the few empirical investigations with the potential to test the popular notion that children's behavior and emotional problems are worsening. They concluded that there are small but pervasive increases in the number of problems exhibited by children, and there are decreases in child competency. Increasingly, problems of society are being felt in the children and are demonstrated by the presence of one or more clinically significant emotional or behavioral problems, identified in 13% to 20% of children (Benard, 1991; Illback, 1994; Kauffman, 1993).

To further complicate matters, issues confronting children and families are complex and often interrelated; a family rarely suffers from one problem in isolation from other problems (Kahne & Kelley, 1993). For instance, a child exhibiting poor academic performance at school often returns to a home characterized by conflict, substance abuse, or the confounding effects of poverty. A response to one need may not negate other remaining problems.

School counselors understand that children who fail in the education system often experience difficulties in other areas of their lives (Soler & Shauffer, 1993). For those students who do fail, the risks of dropping out of school before attaining a high school diploma are associated with higher rates of unemployment; lower earning potential; greater incidence of medical, psychological, and emotional problems; crime; drug abuse; and violence (Post, 1999). If school success is the barometer we use to judge wellness in children, then how do we influence the variables leading to an increase in achievement? Good and Brophy (1986) have claimed that school curriculum, socioeconomic grouping, individual class size, and physical facilities are associated less with pupil progress than with family environment, which is the primary influence. Similarly, in the school setting, a positive school environment (as described by a caring atmosphere, sense of community, and an overall social culture in which students feel they belong and are respected, valued, and welcomed) has the greatest impact on student success. The school counselor is positioned to understand and encourage both the family and the school environment.

Why Intervene at the School Site?

Researchers Braden and Sherrard (1987) discovered that families of children exhibiting school problems are reluctant to seek mental health services in settings outside of schools. This makes a compelling case for counseling families at the school. It is a clear signal for the school counselor's expertise to be exercised. If the school system can become more appealing and encourage these same disenfranchised families to feel more welcome, perhaps more children can be helped. Too, the child benefits when the parents are involved in school issues. Dryfoos observed (1994) that children of absent parents—those parents who do not participate in the school life of their children—suffer most of all.

If schools want to help increase the number of children who succeed in school, and by extension later in life, then they will increasingly need to recognize and deal with other influential factors early in a child's life and not limit their efforts to the individual child in the school setting. Early intervention with children and families, and prevention of future stressors, are the keys to a child's healthy development. Families need to be involved. Schools currently have limited interaction with families, for example, only through parent-teacher conferences. These contacts have limited effects. To have a broader, more permanent impact, the family must be involved at every possible juncture of the school system.

The school counselor is perhaps in the best position to help families because counselors understand the school system, understand the developmental needs of children, and have experience working with many people with mental and behavioral disorders in the school system. Because school attendance is compulsory for all children ages 7 to 16, a school counselor is the mental health professional who is in the unique position for early identification, intervention, and resolution of the difficulties faced by today's children. More organizations are looking to schools as perhaps the only institution that affords direct access to every family with school-aged children to provide the ideal site for systems intervention. Additionally, school counselors' experience in collaboration and consultation with school staff members (i.e., teachers, administration, and staff) and outside referral agencies makes the process of incorporating families into the school setting more seamless than might initially be thought.

Does Family Counseling in Schools Work?

Conventional wisdom suggests that troubled children who behave at school in a way that attracts the attention of a school counselor will benefit from family counseling. Historical tradition can perhaps shed some light. In the early 1950s, John Bowlby, who is largely responsible for present-day attachment theory ideas, grew frustrated in his psychoanalysis with individual children. He decided to bring in the parents for one session but saw these useful family sessions as an adjunct to individual therapy. Child guidance clinics at that time were operating on the premise that treating emotional illness in childhood was the best approach to truncating mental illness in adults. It was child guidance clinicians who concluded that the presenting problem exhibited by the child was more often a reflection of tensions in the family.

Much research ensued because in the 1950s family counseling was a growing approach receiving professional attention from the entire therapy field. Research is more often conducted in clinical settings with inpatients, and at this time a popular research pool for family therapy were families with a member diagnosed with schizophrenia. As more research evolved, individual family members (often the mother) were no longer identified or blamed for the patient's problem, but were simply part of a system that had some disturbance. This shift—from viewing either the child as characterologically disturbed or the parents as toxic influences to viewing the system or interaction among family relationships as flawed—has obvious implications for seeing a child with his or her family in counseling settings. As Nichols and Schwartz (1998) succinctly stated, "Instead of trying—in vain—to separate children from their families, child guidance workers began to help families support their children" (p. 24).

The research on family counseling in school settings is sparse. The actual practice of family counseling in a school is new and not widely adopted. The evolution of school counseling has moved from being a profession of exclusively guidance, academics, and career exploration to one that deals more with interpersonal dilemmas. On the other hand, family counselors typically practice in private or clinical settings, not in schools. These two counseling specialties come together when conducting family counseling in a school setting is proposed. Conducting research on this new practice has not yielded much evidence to date. A chasm exists between the work priorities of researchers and clinicians. Clinicians, especially in school settings, are notorious for having overwhelming workloads and little time for formal research. In addition, school counselors have a preference for working with children and have less interest in conducting empirical studies. The limited studies have discovered support for working with children and their families in school settings. For more on this topic, see chapter 7.

What Family Therapy Studies Have Found

Caution is suggested in interpreting findings from the family therapy literature as well as school counseling efficacy literature. Research in both domains suffers from methodological limitations, lack of effect size, unclear implications for cost benefit, and a limited number of robust studies. No research by professionals conducting family counseling at the school site has been published.

Looking specifically at research on family therapy with children, the following findings are clear:

- Nonbehavioral and behavioral approaches are preferable to no treatment at all, or in 67% of cases (Goldenberg & Goldenberg, 2000; Thompson & Rudolph, 1996).
- Family therapy interventions are more effective than out-of-home placements in 50% of cases. Significant cost benefits can be associated with family therapy more than with out-of-home placements (Thompson & Rudolph, 1996).

Research on family therapy specifically with children exhibiting school problems has shown the following:

- Parent management training (PMT) has shown positive results in reducing targeted behavior problems at home and at school, including up to 14 years later (Nichols & Schwartz, 1998).
- Parent training combined with individual cognitive therapy for the child has been shown to reduce simple phobias, particularly school avoidance (Nichols & Schwartz, 1998).

Studies of indicators of parental involvement and student outcome have found the following:

- When measuring student achievement in school and the effect of parent involvement in school, students demonstrate higher grades, higher test scores, reduced placement in special education or remedial classes, higher graduation rates, and higher enrollment in postsecondary education (Sandell, 1998).
- When measuring student attitudes and behavior and the effect of parental involvement in school, students demonstrate more positive attitude about school and a more positive behavior at school (Sandell, 1998).

School counseling research studies have found the following:

- Group counseling seems to be helpful with elementary children who are experiencing a variety of difficulties, including family distress (Whiston & Sexton, 1998).
- Group counseling seems to be helpful with secondary schoolchildren who are experiencing family adjustment difficulties (Whiston & Sexton, 1998).

Thus in general, family counseling in a school setting—with adult caregivers and their children—conducted by school counselors can be beneficial. However, if counselors want support for programs to work with families in a school setting, they will have to collect data on what they do (process research) as well as on the effects of their efforts (outcome research). School counselors will have to be more vigilant in conducting rigorous studies for these claims to be sustained, although there is ample evidence to indicate that working to support families in school settings on school disturbance is the method of choice.

What Is the Difference Between Parent Consultation and Family Counseling in Schools?

Many school counselors regularly communicate with the families of their students using a consultation approach. Consultation is providing information, presenting instructions, giving suggestions for handling situations, and facilitating planning processes (Schmidt, 1999). The school counselor is seen as the student development specialist. Family counseling involves meeting with a student and as much of his or her family as is deemed important to deal with problems of a more personal nature. Consultation may be seen as a more psychoeducational approach, whereas family counseling in a school setting involves problems of a more personal nature. A school counselor providing family counseling must have the appropriate training in family systems. A family therapy approach would be both more intensive and personal, but it is not the focus of this book.

Are School Counselors Adequately Trained to Offer Family Counseling in a School Setting?

Graduate students enrolled in master's degree programs in institutions accredited by the Council for the Accreditation of Counseling and Related Educational Programs (CACREP) receive similar training and coursework for the majority of their program—regardless of focus—in the form of required courses. Many school counselors receive marriage and family counseling training (Amatea & Fabrick, 1981; DiCocco, 1986; Hinkle, 1993; Peeks, 1993) as part of their program and use a systems approach in the school setting (Lewis, 1996). Family systems counseling is more than just a technique; it is a conceptual change in the way counselors think about people and their difficulties and how to remedy these concerns. School counselors practice in large school systems; systematic processes are familiar. To incorporate the family systems process, school counselors need family counseling course work.

To be effective and to remain within the ethical guideline of operating within their area of competence (American Counseling Association, 1995, Ethical Standard C.2.a), school counselors, operating from a family systems perspective, must focus on the difficulty experienced by the student in the school setting. It may be tempting to look further at family dynamics or problems within the marital relationship and understand that work in those areas may very well increase the success of the student in school. However, couple counseling in all likelihood is beyond the expertise of the school counselor, a time-consuming venture, and not the appropriate focus of the school counselor. Thus the focus of counseling should remain on how the family-school-peer influence can be managed to be supportive of the student and his or her academic success.

The abilities of those who deliver the various components of the counseling intervention must be taken into consideration. No school counselor should conduct family counseling, or operate outside his or her field of expertise, without proper training. Parent consultation, however, is an area in which school counselors are competent. If the school system encourages the families to be more involved, and understands the circular nature of helping families to help children, there must be a willingness on the part of the school board to employ those with the appropriate background or to invest in training existing personnel in family process. Interestingly, marriage and family counselors often never include children in therapy (Korner & Brown, 1990), citing personal comfort level in working with children as a reason (Johnson & Thomas, 1999). A typical school counselor, however, has no such discomfort. Perhaps child development should be a requirement of family counselor training.

Resistance to implementation of family counseling in the school does not reside exclusively with the school counselor. Families regard schools largely as providing academic instruction for their children and may believe that home problems are not the domain of the school counselor. Despite the obstacles to integrating family counseling in school settings, practicing school counselors long have recognized the importance and practicality of working with the family when dealing with the multitude of school problems. Although school counselors have worked on the periphery of family functioning via parent consultation and behavior management of students, it is time for school counselors to center their work with families to encourage maximum results. However, having the appropriate training, time during the school day, and cooperation of both the school and family are enduring challenges.

Setting Up and Conducting a Family Counseling Session: A Five-Step Model

The family counseling process is similar to the individual counseling process: building a relationship, the working phase of counseling, and appropriate termination. The school counselor must develop rapport with the family, just as he or she does with the individual student. Typically, counseling a family follows this pattern: developing rapport with all family members, conducting the working phase, consulting and following up, and terminating therapy. As with all counseling sessions, being conscious of the content (what is actually said, both verbally and nonverbally) and the process (the flow of information and direction of session) is essential.

In an individual session, the counselor is concerned with both what the student says and the progress or growth of the student. Balanced, fruitful sessions move toward the goal established by the counselee. Good counselors know that if they pay no attention to the process of counseling, the session effectively gets derailed and becomes bogged down in detail or spirals out of emotional control. Equally, if the process is the greatest concern, the client does not feel attended to or heard if all efforts are concentrated on getting through the sessions. In the model (see Figure 1.1) of counseling presented here, process and content of sessions are like railroad tracks. To achieve the goals of counseling (to ensure the train arrives successfully at its destination), the practitioner must attend to both the process (i.e., the movement of the session) and the content (i.e., what is said verbally and nonverbally). Process and content form the structure or train track for counseling; both rails are necessary for balanced movement toward mutually agreed-upon goals. A family counselor must be attentive to the process—mak-

FIGURE 1.1
Railroad Model of Counseling

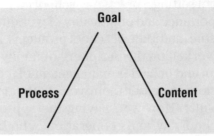

ing sure everyone is on board—as well as the content—making sure everyone gets a chance to be heard.

In this railroad metaphor, as Figure 1.2 illustrates, each cross-tie along the track holds the two rails together and facilitates the progressive movement of the counseling cycle. The first cross-ties contribute to the development of rapport (Steps 1, 2, and 3). If these are successfully negotiated, the family (train) working with the coun-

FIGURE 1.2
Five-Step Counseling Model for Home/
School Intervention

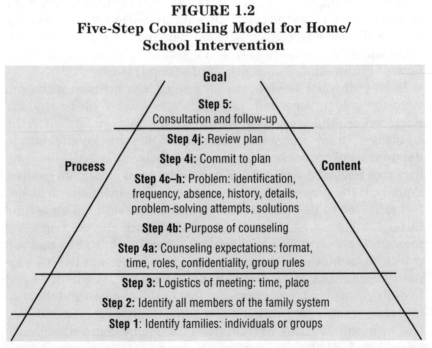

Steps 1–3 are the relationship-building phase, Step 4 is the working phase, and Step 5 is the termination phase.

selor (engineer) can move down the tracks to the working phase (Step 4) and eventually toward termination (Step 5).

The five steps of the counseling model for home/school intervention use this progressive railroad scheme to illustrate the counseling process (each step) and content (questions and topics to be addressed at each step). The relationship-building phase (Steps 1, 2, and 3) of counseling with a family entails identifying the target population and arranging logistics for the meeting.

Step 1: Identify the Possible Families for Single-Family Counseling or Multiple-Family Counseling

If a school counselor wishes to deal with a certain difficulty experienced by several children (e.g., homework habits, lack of attendance), using a group format for several families can be beneficial. Remember that the focus is on the difficulty, not the child or the particular family. This type of counseling is known as either family demonstration (i.e., each week a family volunteers to receive counseling in front of a group of families regarding normal, developmental concerns) or multiple-family group counseling (i.e., the same families are brought together every week for group sessions).

Benefits of the group approach to family counseling are similar to the benefits for individuals involved in group counseling. Given a counselor's limited time, the group approach has an obvious benefit of time efficiency. Resistance is often lower in a group format because the focus is not on an individual family. The generalizable effects are considerable as families realize they are not alone in dealing with difficulties. They can feel less isolated. They may get more ideas from others as they search for solutions.

If the problem involves a more complex issue, or if the counselor feels that the family would be more appropriately seen, or more likely to participate, in the privacy of the counselor's office, then a single family can be seen in a counselor's office. The focus is on childhood or family life-cycle developmental concerns and contributing to the success of the child in the school setting.

Step 2: Identify All Members of the System

It is critical that the counselor identify all the players of the system that involves the child: the family, school, or family-school subsystems. The inclusion of various people who are in a position to recognize, support, and influence the system is crucial. Systems theorists strongly believe that all members play a role, often unwittingly, in contributing to the development and maintenance of a particular problem. It is key to have everyone involved in solution finding. Everyone is needed in the session because, more often than not, family members do not realize how they perpetuate problem behavior in the child, or symptom bearer, and need to be alerted to their participation in problem maintenance.

The following scenario provides an example.

> When Chloe stays at Dad's house, they stay up late because they are catching up with each other and because Dad works a late shift. Chloe oversleeps, Dad calls the attendance office to excuse the behavior, and Dad's girlfriend drives Chloe to school. Dad and girlfriend may feel that they are doing their job by spending time with Chloe and getting the child to school, but their actions reassure Chloe that she can sleep in at no great inconvenience. Thus, Dad and girlfriend contribute unknowingly to Chloe's lackadaisical attitude toward school. When Chloe returns the next week to live at Mom's house, the first-period teacher telephones to alert Mom of Chloe's poor participation grade caused by excessive tardiness and absences. Mom quickly determines that the tardy classes coincide with Chloe's weeks at Dad's house. Mom contacts Dad and rants about his poor parenting, lack of consistency, academic implications, and so forth. Dad is defensive and angrily accuses Mom of meddling. Chloe hears all of this and vows not to let one parent know anything about the other parent. This burden of concentrating on saying the correct thing in both homes affects Chloe's concentration on schoolwork, contributing to poorer classroom performance by Chloe. All members of this family are contributing to Chloe's negative academic performance.

Perhaps the greatest challenge is convincing the nonschool family members (e.g., older siblings, parents, extended family) that the school is the most appropriate place to deal with the various problems presented by the child in the school or home setting. The school counselor must be sensitive to feelings of reluctance, perhaps even hostility, toward the school. Likewise, school counselors must not presume a traditional family model for participants. Many cultures honor people who participate in different roles in families, and who may or may not be related by blood. The family needs to determine the influential participants.

Step 3: Set a Meeting Time

The establishment of a meeting time that is convenient for all participants can be trying. As the vast majority of parents work outside the home, schedule conflicts are to be expected. Patience and flexibility are welcome assets in determining a family and counselor meeting time. For those families who absolutely cannot take time off during the school day, or cannot afford the time off, consider alternate meeting times. This may, at first glance, be more than the school counselor can tackle. However, the payoff occurs when the student begins to perform up to expectations and relieves the counselor of time devoted to that particular student.

Parents also may be reluctant to come in the evening. Suggest a before-school or before-work meeting (e.g., 7:00 a.m.). This may be inconvenient for counselors, but most families have a difficult time refusing an early morning appointment. Secondary schools often use this strategy for disciplinary matters. Perhaps a meeting time immediately after the workday can be managed, before heading home (e.g., 5:00 p.m.). Consider, too, one Saturday each month for family conferencing. This may be allowed in school district contracts as "comp" time.

Step 4: Facilitate the Meeting

This is the working phase for the counselor, student, and family. The counselor meets with the family to begin establishing rapport by defining the problem and clarifying expectations. Next, all participants explore what has been done to solve the problem, brainstorm or explore new solutions, narrow options, and finally commit to and implement new options. Sometimes this counseling phase may proceed during one appointment, or it may be set as a series of appointments.

Discuss meeting format. The counselor begins by explaining the process of family counseling. This includes detailing the role of each person (including facilitator), the time parameters and expectations involved, issues of confidentiality,[1] and the possibility and scheduling of follow-up sessions (if needed). Often families are unfamiliar with the assumed elements of counseling. This discussion of client rights sets the tone of equality and lends an atmosphere of respect and expectations.

It is important to establish rules such as "No put downs," "Everyone gets a chance to talk," and "Respectful attitude shown at all times." If a participant gets emotional or hostile, it is best to remind the person of the commitment to the rules. It is quite easy for a family discussion to escalate into shouting. It is better, of course, to establish expectations of behavior in the beginning of the meeting.

Identify the purpose. "Why are we here?" Let the student speak first, followed by each family member. The counselor summarizes the family's ideas. Watch for overbearing or dominating family members, and control input. The counselor needs to reinforce ideas of equality (everyone gets a chance to speak and offer his or her opinion) and safety (the overall purpose is to help the student be more successful in school, with the problems discussed fairly and respect shown for all).

Children may offer resistance to a family session, in the form of silence. This may reflect unfamiliarity with the counseling process or an innocent lack of comprehension of their role in the meeting. It could signal more negative ideas as well, such as a fear of reprisal from a feared or strongly opinionated family member. It is best to speak with the student at length before the family session, to explain the format of the meeting, and to find out if problems of neglect or abuse are suspected or present. If abuse or neglect is suspected, the counselor will have to make the appropriate report to the authorities and evaluate the appropriateness of working with the remaining family members in a session.

If the child is simply quiet, encourage the child to speak by emphasizing safety and positive communication. Play therapy (e.g., using art, clay, games, and coloring) may be beneficial. What will ensure silence is an overly talkative adult in the session. Use of a talking stick (i.e., any prop that can be handed from participant to participant) can help regulate and limit who does the talking.

Determine the problem. Everyone states his or her views. The counselor should ask for concrete examples and use open-ended questions. Help the family externalize or objectify the problem. That is, reframe negative comments about a person to behaviors that are unacceptable. Rather than "She is moody and defiant," say "Her mood can be erratic and her attitude is defiant," or for younger children, "The 'Moody Monster' has been visiting her frequently."

Occasionally a counselor may wonder if a child or parent is telling the truth when a dramatic difference in stories appears. Anyone may fabricate or embellish the truth to elicit sympathy or exaggerate to get attention. The counselor is advised to use gentle confrontation or admit concern, saying, "I am not really clear about what happened. Perhaps you can tell me more." This may make the session feel awkward and uncomfortable, but exaggerations can be expected. The dishonesty develops from an underlying misunderstanding or fear.

Determine when the problem occurs. The counselor should direct the family to be specific. People tend to talk in extremes or make global statements (e.g., "He *always* acts aggressively," or "My mom *is forever* working late"). Find out exactly when the behavior manifests itself. Can triggers (e.g., events, teachers, peers, time of day) be detailed? Get the specific context. It may be helpful to scale the behavior (e.g., "On a scale of 1 to 10, 1 being the problem is completely dominating the morning and 10 being the problem is no longer noticed, how would you rate the problem today?").

Learn the history of the problem. Again, families may want to dwell on the history behind the problem. That is not what is intended here. The history in this model seeks to determine if other factors can be implicated in the behavior disturbance. For instance, if a child has fairly recently begun exhibiting aggressive tendencies, it may coincide with a recent loss (e.g., divorce, separation, death of pet or family member, residential move). Questions regarding the temporal quality, or time element, look for other system factors, rather than behavior demonstrated by the student in isolation. Try to reframe behavior as a well-intentioned, if misguided, attempt to negotiate family or life-cycle events (e.g., "You thought that failing geography might be a way to get your mom to talk to your dad about you, rather than fighting about their marriage").

Be aware of the perception of personal inferiority. Children generally are not born with innate ideas of wanting to disappoint parents, teachers, and others of importance in their lives. Hearing negative comments engenders feelings of inferiority and contributes to feelings of inadequacy, inferiority, and lack of competence. Reframing intentions, avoiding global statements of failure, and focusing on strengths will avoid this.

Adlerians promote the education of parents (and, if appropriate, mature children) on the four goals of misbehavior: attention, power, revenge, and display of inadequacy (Dinkmeyer & McKay, 1993). One technique to use with teens is to simply ask if the behavior was an attempt to reach a goal of misbehavior (e.g., "Were you doing this to gain attention, even though it was negative?" or "Did you want to get back at Mom for moving you out of your last school as a sort of revenge?").

Determine when the problem does not occur. This is a classic behavior modification technique. The solution-focused theorists have adopted this and call it *checking for exceptions*. Pay attention to what is happening at home and school when the behavior is absent. This is also a gentle reminder for all parties that the good behavior is being overlooked and must be acknowledged and remembered. Family members need to catch the child being good.

Find out about prior attempts to solve the problem. Counselors often forget to credit families with a history of working on the problem or already trying to implement strategies to address the trouble. Identify, capitalize on, and reinforce family strengths. Demonstrate respect for parental past attempts and authority. Some family theorists (e.g., strategic school) believe family troubles are maintained merely by repeatedly using the same flawed solution. If all a person has is a hammer in his or her toolbox, all things begin to look like a nail. Perhaps the hammer has become ineffective in working with that situation or child.

Determine what seems to work and what does not work. Reinforce the idea that if something does not work, parents should not keep repeating the same solution in the hope that it will eventually work. Brainstorm other solutions or successes in other areas. Counselors should explore all options to be sure the family has reviewed basic interventions. Some alternate solutions might be the following:

- Implement a reasonable schedule (for meals, sleep, homework, etc.). Teens have been found to get less sleep than adults at a time in life when more sleep is required. Adults average 7.5 to 8 hours per night, and teens require 1.5 to 2 hours more per night than adults, for a total teen sleep time of 9 to 10 hours each night. All people perform better with predictable schedules. School starts at a regular time, thus homework should have an established time, and meals should be eaten at routine times, if possible. Establish a schedule in the session and chart it together.
- Emphasize consistent supervision. Remind everyone that it is much more difficult to supervise children consistently. It is much easier to punish a child, for example, for not doing homework. Establishing a homework hour and supervising that hour is often the last thing an adult wants to do at the end of the day, but it ultimately results in skill development (good study habits) for the child and a greater chance of success.
- Establish clear communication regarding expectations, responsibilities, and consequences of misbehavior. Parents need to explain clearly their expectations of child behavior. As children

get older, parents assume that their kids will know the rules of the house, either generalizing from older siblings or from general discussions. Each child needs to have an individual conference regarding rules and expectations. This can occur repeatedly. This is a good time to use the redundancy principle: Expectations, consequences, and rewards[2] can never be clearly stated often enough. The best times, for these parent-child conferences are planned, in advance, and occur when the household is calm. Family meetings, scheduled on a weekly basis, can be times to review expectations and to see if anything needs to be renegotiated. Both the parent and the child can look forward to a regular, consistent, positive, and friendly meetings.

A metaphor may underscore the importance of regularly talking about expectations and consequences to children: When we bring children home from the hospital immediately after birth, we put them in a car seat, which is safe and developmentally appropriate. They start out sleeping in a cradle, and when they start to turn over, the cradle is replaced with a crib (safe and developmentally appropriate). When the child grows out of the crib, a big bed is used. Similarly, a family's yard is fenced, or if in an urban setting, a child has boundaries that cannot be crossed, to establish the parameters of exploration. Parents continue to expand the limits of the child's world according to the developmental phase of the child and the safety concerns. When the child is older, parents often forget to explain the boundary or the limitation on behavior. Even though these boundaries are increasingly psychological, the child may not realize the parents' expectation of the established limit, again set according to the developmental phase of the child and the safety concerns. Likewise, the consequences of violating these established expectations and limits need to be discussed and negotiated in a calm manner. In a time of crisis, typically not much is negotiated or explained well. Parents often overreact, and children often become defensive and defiant. Clear expectations and consequences discussed in advance avoid confusion.

- Encourage the family to plan stress-free time together and time apart. Remind families to plan time together in which everyone has a chance to choose what to do or to contribute to what is done. This can be time together every day (such as a mealtime, or a child and a parent preparing dinner together), or time at special events, such as Friday night video and pizza. Encourag-

ing time together in a nonconflictual setting supports caring behavior and family interest.

- Remember other resources to be used as support. For instance,
a favorite teacher or coach (or projects, events, people) can
be part of the intervention. This person can agree to spend
time with the child as a positive consequence for the child
and family staying committed to the program. A person from
the community (e.g., church, self-help group, adult's office)
can be part of the counseling process and intervention. An
anger management group, parenting group, a group for families of children with attention deficit-hyperactivity disorder
(ADHD), or other self-help group may be a source of additional support for the family.
- Get a commitment. Have the family set goals. Remember to
think in terms of small successes, rather than simply long-
term goals (e.g., attending 80% of classes with a long-term
goal of 100% attendance or increasing grade point average
from a 1.3 to a 2.0 with a long-term goal of 3.5). Choose one
solution to attempt to modify behavior and get a consensus
from all members to commit to implementation. Record these
commitments. Encourage adherence to the plan, even if every member does not consistently comply with the plan or if
attempts are unsuccessful.
- Create a review plan for the coming week. Make sure the family
agrees to all parts of the plan and prominently displays it some-
where in the home (e.g., on the refrigerator door). This concrete
representation of commitment is needed. This newly formed
plan is competing with well-established habits, lifestyles, and
other modes of operation that are familiar to the members of
that family. It is exciting to participate in counseling and to
talk about problems. The work comes at home, where counselors want to encourage change and foster accountability.
The written plan reminds members of their commitment to
this process. A written structure or plan is necessary.
- End the session. Ask, "Is there anything else you would like
to add?" Review the commitments of each member and set
the appointment for the next meeting

Step 5: Perform Consultation and Follow-Up

Depending on the nature and severity of the concern, and the
progress made in the initial session, a counselor needs to pay
attention to reinforcing positive family change. Follow-up may be

conducted with the student individually in the counselor's office, over the phone with the family, or with another family session.

If the family appears to be successful, the counselor is advised to check briefly on student progress at a later date. This is simply good case management. If the family feels as if it has progressed but needs more reinforcement, the counselor is advised to continue seeing the family, with a limited number of sessions in mind. If the family appears to be unsuccessful, the counselor can consider consultation with another professional or can refer the family for more intensive counseling or therapy.

Case notes should be written and kept in a confidential file. When writing notes, counselors are reminded of the Family Educational Rights Act of 1974 (FERPA), which allows a parent or legal guardian access to any information relevant to the educational progress of his or her child. Good case noting makes for good practice.

Obstacles to Success

When incorporating family counseling in the schools, counselors may encounter obstacles in relation to both school and family issues.

School issues. School administration must see family counseling at the school site not only as valuable but also as critical. School administration must also be supportive (in terms of space, time, respect for programming issues, encouragement of families, and allotment of counselor's duties). It is the counselor's job to influence the administration. Advocacy efforts are supported by recent research that has revealed the connections between family environment and student success.

The school counselor must feel confident in working with families. Even though he or she may not have couples or family training, the counselor is experienced in dealing with problems that schoolchildren exhibit. This must be maintained as the focus of the counseling. School counseling continues to be a different subspecialty from family counseling. A school counselor must seek additional training in family systems approaches to become fully competent in this area.

Physical space must be available to accommodate families. A school counselor's office—before, during, and after school—may not be able to hold several adults and children comfortably. When moving to space in the school building other than a private office, issues of confidentiality must be addressed. Some venues—for instance, the library—may accommodate several people in a family but may provide distractions or less privacy.

Scheduling issues need to be addressed, both during the school day (e.g., taking a child away from class time for family counseling) and for the rest of the family, who will be altering their schedules to come to the school.

Family issues. Families may feel intimidated by the school setting, personnel, or culture. This needs to be addressed so that the family feels supported. Not all adults were successful in their own experiences with the school system, and they can carry that history with them as parents of schoolchildren.

The family may be in so much upheaval that it may be impossible for the counselor to see all family members for all counseling sessions. Family counseling relies heavily on full participation of all relevant members, so this must be addressed and, depending on the stance of the counselor, stressed.

Scheduling and transportation conflicts may need to be discussed. The counselor may need to be prepared to offer counseling outside the established hours of the traditional school day. Counselors may also consider counseling the family in their home. If this is more practical, counselors must ensure their own safety.

Telephone conferencing, video communication, and even e-mail may play a part in family counseling. Although these vehicles offer much in the way of convenience, this book is concerned with face-to-face family counseling.

Families may not understand their role in helping the child do well academically. When a child is in elementary school, opportunities to be involved at the school may seem more obvious than when a child enters older grades. Throughout all grades, however, research has indicated that the more parents are involved both in a child's education and school life, the greater the outcomes for that child. Increases can be seen in school achievement, interactions with school personnel, standardized scores, participation in school events, communications between home and school, attendance rates, and variables that contribute to positive school climate (Achenbach & Howell, 1993; Illback, 1994; Squires & Kranyik, 1995). Although these connections may be obvious for the school counselor, he or she needs to translate education jargon into effective messages for families. A good counselor will have a list of practical suggestions to offer families regarding how to be more involved with their child's academic life.

Conclusion

Children often come to school troubled. When these troubles interfere with academic performance or attract the concern of school professionals, a school counselor is often the only person in the child's environment who may be in a position to offer psychosocial support to that child. Studies have consistently demonstrated that children do better in academic settings when they have a commitment from and positive communication with their families. Ironically, however, parents or other family members do not always recognize that they contribute to the child's troubles. Healthy family functioning often is only seen on television, and these models may indeed be questionable. The school counselor in a family counseling approach can bridge these two worlds—the school and the family. The advantage of integrating the school and the family systems over mutual concerns of the child can be significant.

A school counselor engaging in family counseling must feel competent, have the appropriate training, operate within his or her area of expertise, and have a commitment to cybernetic change. A good counselor is always aware of the process and content of counseling sessions. Counseling families in the school setting challenges both process and content for a counselor used to working with a child as an individual entity. Family counseling in a school setting is a relatively new approach, but it offers a service that good school counselors have long recognized: To be effective with children, counselors need to be effective with and supported by the family.

Notes

[1] Regarding issues of confidentiality in the United States: Each state uniquely determines the age of majority. Although students are persons and enjoy fundamental rights and freedoms protected by the U. S. Constitution (including rights to confidentiality), the law in all states stipulates that persons under the age of 18 are not adults and, therefore, are not competent to make fully informed voluntary decisions. Furthermore, FERPA, or the Buckley Amendment, states that privacy rights legally belong to the parents or guardians in the context of educational documents. Therefore, student/minor rights are a complicated issue, and a savvy counselor is advised seriously to consider these rights (Miller, 1999).

[2] Regarding the positive effects of rewards: Studies support the idea that rewards can be better than no feedback at all, but they usually lead to decreased intrinsic interest in the task involved. The research on the negative effects of rewards has been more salient and conclusive. Extrinsic rewards, especially if expected, reduce natural interest in a task.

Some studies have suggested that if rewards are used in an autonomous rather than controlling orientation, they can lead to both motivation and increased self-esteem. According to Zabrzezny (1989), role modeling, pleasant environment, opportunities to feel successful, meaningful lessons in punishment and rewards, clear communication and expectations, verbal praise, immediate feedback, and providing choices encourage autonomy.

References

Achenbach, T. M., & Howell, C. T. (1993). Are American children's problems getting worse? A 13-year comparison. *Journal of the American Academy of Child and Adolescent Psychiatry, 32,* 1145–1154.

Amatea, E., & Fabrick, P. (1981). Family systems counseling: A position alternative to traditional counseling. *Elementary School Guidance and Counseling, 15,* 228–236.

American Counseling Association. (1995). *Code of ethics and standards of practice.* Alexandria, VA: Author.

Benard, B. (1991). *Fostering resiliency in kids: Protective factors in the family, school, and community.* Boulder, CO: Prevention Center.

Braden, J. P., & Sherrard, P.A.D. (1987). Referring families to nonschool agencies: A family systems approach. *School Psychology Review, 16,* 513–518.

DiCocco, B. (1986). A guide to family/school intervention for the family therapist. *Contemporary Family Therapy, 8,* 50–61.

Diller, L. (1991). Not seen and not heard. *The Family Therapy Networker, 15,* 18–27.

Dinkmeyer, D., & McKay, G. (1993). *Systematic training for effective parenting.* Circle Pines, MN: American Guidance Service.

Doherty, W. J., & Simmons, D. S. (1996). Clinical practice patterns of marriage and family therapists: A national survey of therapists and their clients. *Journal of Marital and Family Therapy, 22*(1), 9–25.

Dryfoos, J. G. (1994). *Full-service Schools: A revolution in health and social services for children, youth, and families.* San Francisco: Jossey-Bass.

Forgatch, M. S., & Patterson, G. R. (1998). Behavior family therapy. In F. M. Dattilio (Ed.), *Case studies in couple and family therapy: Systemic and cognitive perspectives.* New York: Guilford Press.

Goldenberg, I., & Goldenberg, H. (2000). *Family therapy: An overview.* Pacific Grove, CA: Brooks/Cole.

Good, T. L., & Brophy, J. E. (1986). School effects. In M. C. Wittrock (Ed.), *Handbook of research on teaching* (3rd ed., pp. 570–602). New York: Macmillan.

Harter, S. (1993). Causes and consequences of low self-esteem in children and adolescents. In R. Baumeister (Ed.), *Self-esteem: The puzzle of low self-regard.* New York: Plenum Press.

Hinkle, S. (1993). Training school counselors to do family therapy. *Elementary School Guidance and Counseling, 27*, 252–257.

Illback, R. (1994). Poverty and the crisis in children's services: The need for services integration. *Journal of Clinical Child Psychology, 23*, 413, 424.

Johnson, L., & Thomas, V. (1999). Influences on the inclusion of children in family therapy. *Journal of Marital and Family Therapy, 25*(1), 117–123.

Kahne, J., & Kelley, C. (1993). Assessing the coordination of children's services: Dilemmas facing program administration, evaluation and policy analysts. *Education and Urban Society, 25*, 187–200.

Kale, A., & Landreth, G. (1999). Filial therapy with parents of children experiencing learning difficulties. *International Journal of Play Therapy, 8*(2), 35–56.

Kauffman, J. M. (1993). *Characteristics of emotional and behavioral disorders of children and youth.* New York: Macmillan.

Korner, S., & Brown, G. (1990). Exclusion of children from psychotherapy: Family therapists' beliefs and practices. *Journal of Family Psychology, 3*(4), 420–430.

Lewis, W. (1996). A proposal for initiating family counseling interventions by school counselors. *The School Counselor, 44*, 93–99.

Miller, L. (1999). Working with families and children in school settings. In P. Stevens (Ed.), *Ethical casebook for the practice of marriage and family counselors.* Alexandria, VA: American Counseling Association.

Nichols, M. P., & Schwartz, R. C. (1998). *Family therapy: Concepts and methods.* Needham Heights, MA: Allyn & Bacon.

Peeks, B. (1993). Revolutions in counseling and education: A systems perspective in the schools. *Elementary School Guidance and Counseling, 27*, 245–251.

Post, P. (1999). Impact of child-centered play therapy on the self-esteem, locus of control, and anxiety of at-risk 4th, 5th, and 6th grade students. *International Journal of Play Therapy, 8*(2), 1–18.

Sandell, E. (1998). Parents in the schools. In M. L. Fuller & G. Olsen (Eds.), *Home-school relations.* Boston: Allyn & Bacon.

Schmidt, J. J. (1999). *Counseling in schools: Essential services and comprehensive programs* (3rd ed.). Boston: Allyn & Bacon.

Soler, M., & Shauffer, C. (1993). Fighting fragmentation: Coordination of services for children and families. *Education and Urban Society, 25*, 129–140.

Squires, D. A., & Kranyik, R. D. (1995, December/January). The Comer program: Changing school culture. *Educational Leadership,* 29–32.

Stith, S. M., Rosen, K. H., McCollum, E. E., & Herman, S. A. (1996). The voices of children: Preadolescent children's experiences in family therapy. *Journal of Marital and Family Therapy, 22*, 69–86.

Thompson, C. L., & Rudolph, L. B. (1996). *Counseling children.* Pacific Grove, CA: Brooks/Cole.

Whiston, S. C., & Sexton, T. L. (1998). A review of school counseling out-
come research: Implications for practice. *Journal of Counseling &
Development, 76,* 412–426.
Zbrezny, R. A. (1989). *Effects of extrinsic rewards on intrinsic motiva-
tion: Improving learning in elementary classrooms.* (ERIC Document
Reproduction Service No. ED309870)

■ ■ ■

2

Working With Families: A Rationale for School Counseling Programs

William G. Nicoll, PhD

Family dynamics and parental involvement have been consistently identified as key factors influencing children's academic success and social adjustment. In their review of the research on student achievement, Good and Brophy (1986) concluded that the research to date indicates family factors account for more of the variance in student achievement than do curricular and instructional variables. A recent national longitudinal study on adolescent health concluded that both family and school social contexts are associated with health and risky behaviors in adolescents. In particular, parent-family connectedness and perceived school connectedness were found to be protective against every major health risk behavior measure for adolescents, including suicidality, violence, substance abuse, tobacco use, and emotional distress (Resnick et al., 1997). The researchers concluded that health professionals, social service providers, and educators must begin to take steps to diminish the risk factors and enhance protective factors for our youth. Programs focused on preventive and early intervention services with families could greatly enhance students' academic success and social adjustment as well as increase parental involvement and support for the school itself.

Henderson and Berla (1995) concluded from their review of family–school effects research that there is strong evidence documenting that when schools provide support to families, children realize benefits such as higher grades and test scores, better school attendance, fewer special education placements, more positive attitudes and behavior, higher graduation rates, and increased enrollment in postsecondary education. In addition, Henderson and Berla also pointed out that research has demonstrated that schools and communities also benefit from such family-focused school programs through improved teacher morale, higher ratings of teachers by parents, more support from families, higher student achievement, and better reputations in the community.

In light of such findings linking family dynamics to children's school success, two of the eight National Education Goals stress the importance of family factors in children's education. Goal One states that all children should start school "ready to learn" and notes that parents are the child's first teachers and need to assist their preschool children in developing this readiness. Goal Eight states directly that every school will promote partnerships that increase parental involvement and participation to promote the social, emotional, and academic growth of children (National Educational Goals Panel, 1994). Yet, as Susan McAllister Swap (1993) has since noted,

> Given the widespread recognition that parent involvement in schools is important, that it is unequivocally related to improvement in children's achievement and that improvement in children's achievement is urgently needed, it is paradoxical that most schools do not have a comprehensive parent involvement program. (p. 12)

Although most educators and researchers support the educational policy direction of increasing parent involvement, few agree as to what constitutes effective involvement (Baker & Soden, 1998), and fewer still seem to be actively seeking to initiate comprehensive programs.

Counselors working directly in the schools are ideally situated to coordinate and provide such comprehensive family–school programs. Counseling interventions for child and adolescent difficulties are far more effective when directed at altering interaction patterns of the significant adults in the child's life. Parent education and parent-teacher resource centers, along with a family systems approach to counseling, consultation, and intervention services, appear to be ideal strategies for increasing the visibility and effectiveness of school counselors while simultaneously providing optimal services to the school community. Yet, school counselors typically do not receive significant training in family counseling during their professional preparation courses, and fewer still actively initiate a comprehensive family counseling and family involvement component into their comprehensive school counseling program. Indeed, most models for developing comprehensive school counseling programs ignore or minimize the counselor's function in working with parents and families (e.g., Dahir, Sheldon, & Valiga, 1998; Gysbers & Henderson, 1988; Myrick, 1993; Walz, 1988). Clearly, the current state of the art in school counseling programs is out of sync with the research base on the importance of family dynamics and children's social and academic achievement.

This chapter, therefore, reviews the research literature regarding family dynamics and student achievement to establish an empirically sound rationale for establishing a family-focused component within existing school counseling programs. Following the review, key components of a family-focused school counseling program are delineated for possible program redesign and development.

Family Involvement and Achievement

From birth to age 18, children spend only 9% of their time in school (White-Clark & Decker, 1996). Parents obviously, therefore, play a crucial role in the development of intelligence, achievement, and academic competence in their children because much of the remaining 91% of children's lives consist mainly of parental and family interactions. Research has consistently highlighted the importance of the family in determining children's school success and social adjustment.

Children whose parents are involved in educational activities at home or in school activities achieve more in school, regardless of socioeconomic status (Benson, Buckley, & Medrich, 1980). Achievement test scores have been found to vary directly with the number of hours parents spend involved in activities related to the school program (Irvine, 1979). Parents of high achievers visit their children's school more often, get acquainted with the teachers, and become involved in school activities. Parents of high achievers also are found to set high standards for their children's educational activities and maintain a home environment that supports learning. These parents are more involved in home learning activities, and their children spend more time on homework (Clark, 1993).

Children in elementary school are more likely than children in middle or high school to have parents who are highly involved in their school (Dauber & Epstein, 1993; Nord, 1998). However, Dauber and Epstein (1993) also found that the level of parent involvement is directly correlated to the specific practices that schools and teachers use to encourage involvement at school and to guide parents in how to help their children at home. Important types of parental involvement that have been found to affect student success include:

- providing a stimulating environment that emphasizes literacy;
- holding high expectations for school and home performance, with moderate levels of parental support and supervision;
- monitoring homework completion and reinforcing of school assignments;
- emphasizing effort more than ability;
- engaging in practices that promote independence and problem-solving strategies;
- frequently responding to and interacting with children; and
- acting as models of learning and achievement (Baker & Soden, 1998; Becher, 1984; Dauber & Epstein, 1993; Williams, 1994).

Deslandes, Royer, and Turcotte (1997) in a study of 525 ninth-grade students found that parental involvement in terms of affective support, communication with teachers, and family discussions regarding school, grades, and achievement was positively correlated with school grades. Further, they found that improved school grades were also associated with the adolescent's perception of parents as being firm, warm, involved, and democratic (i.e., authoritative). Similarly, Hickman, Greenwood, and Miller (1995) found that among high school students parent involvement was correlated with grade point average when involvement included active support, communication with the school regarding the child's progress, advocacy, and home-based learning activities. However, parental involvement that included volunteering at the school and serving on school committees did not seem to affect student grade point average.

In a study by Clark (1993) involving more than 1,100 elementary-age students, findings indicated that parents of high achievers were more involved in home learning activities, and their children spent more time on homework. Interestingly, parents of low achievers assisted their children with homework more but spent less time on home learning. High achievers came from a wide variety of family backgrounds, but in all cases parents typically set high standards for their children's educational activities and maintained a home environment supportive of learning.

Benson, Buckley, and Medrich (1980) gathered data from parents of 764 sixth graders to examine the relationship between specific parent–child interactions and school performance. They concluded that elementary school children whose parents spend time with them in educational activities achieve more in school, regardless of socioeconomic status, although the effects of different types of activities are different for low-income children versus middle- or high-income children. Unlike children in higher income families, low-income students did not show any positive effect on achievement for going to cultural activities. Across all socioeconomic groups, however, parental encouragement of hobbies, participation in organized activities, family dinner times, and family activities on weekends were found to be the most powerful family parent–child interaction predictors of academic achievement.

A study of extremely talented young professionals from difficult competitive fields conducted to determine common factors that might predict such future success indicated that the most common characteristic impacting the professionals' general education, specialized training, and achievement was enthusiastic parent involvement (Bloom, 1985). Parent enthusiasm was the main confirmation that the goals the professionals were pursuing were entirely worthwhile and fully within their reach.

Similar to Bloom's findings, Caplan, Choy, and Whitmore (1992) conducted a study of academically successful Southeast Asian children who immigrated to the United States in the late 1970s and early 1980s and found that high academic success can be traced to strong family values regarding the importance of education and a home environment that supports learning. Caplan, Choy, and Whitmore noted in their results that several significant values and family practices were correlated with high achievement. These included parents reading aloud to their children, homework dominating weeknight activities, relative equality existing between the sexes, a love of learning being present, parents holding a strong belief in the children's potential to master their own destinies, and parents placing an emphasis on education as the key to social acceptance and economic success. Encouragement of academic rigor and excellence led to high achievement. These researchers concluded that when families instill a respect for education and create a home environment that encourages learning, children do better in school.

Although the importance of parental involvement has been clearly established in the research, there is wide variance among parents and schools in regard to parent involvement. More highly educated parents and parents with higher socioeconomic status are more likely to be actively involved in their children's schools (Vaden-Kiernan & Davis, 1993; Zill & Nord, 1994). However, school policies and teacher practices are significant factors influencing the level of parental involvement in children's education (Eccles & Harold, 1996; Epstein, 1990). It is likely that less educated parents and parents who themselves had negative school experiences are intimidated by, or reluctant to become actively involved in, their children's school. Thus, counselors, teachers, and administrators must work to develop policies and practices that actively encourage all parents to become involved and that diminish the inhibiting factors that prevent some parents from actively participating.

Parenting Style and Achievement

Although the quantity of parent involvement in children's school experience and learning activities has been much discussed as a key contributor to children's academic and social success, the quality of the parent–child relationship may be even more important. The family's main contribution to success in school is made through the parent–child relationship (Nicoll, 1991, 1992, 1994). The nature of this relationship can have either a positive or adverse impact on student achievement. As early as 1951, early reading success was correlated with family interaction patterns, such as communication patterns, expression of positive affect, parental discipline styles, and home socialization practices (Milner, 1951). Fifty years of subsequent research has provided clear and convincing evidence of the powerful role family dynamics play in children's school success, indeed even more powerful than school instructional variables (Ferguson, 1991; Good & Brophy, 1986).

Characteristic parent–child interaction patterns—that is, parenting style—appear to be the most powerful family variable influencing children's academic success and social adjustment. Baumrind's (1967, 1975) original three parenting style typology has been more recently expanded to a typology of four basic parenting styles: authoritarian, authoritative, permissive-indulgent, and permissive-disengaged (Darling, 1999; Maccoby & Martin, 1983; Nicoll, 1991, 1992). Authoritarian (or autocratic) parents are defined as being highly demanding and directive but providing little positive emotional support. Such parents seek to shape and control the child's behaviors and attitudes and focus on behavior control, or compliance as parenting strategies (e.g., reward and punishment). Authoritative parents establish clear standards and expectations of their children and also use supportive rather than punitive disciplinary methods. Such parents take a strong, active interest in the totality of their children's lives, setting reasonable, firm limits without being intrusive and overly controlling. A positive, respectful, and encouraging relationship is maintained, and children are expected to assume responsibility in their lives. The permissive-indulgent parenting style involves a high level of responsiveness by the parent but a low level of limit and boundary setting. Such parents place a high value on making the child's life happy and tend to avoid firm limits and expectations for responsible, respectful behavior. The permissive-disengaged parenting style is described as being low on both parental responsiveness and parental demands. Children are left to self-regulate their behavior and activities, and the parent shows little or no interest in the child as an individual, fulfilling primarily the instrumental care-taking roles of providing food, clothing, and shelter but not the essential affective support.

Probably the most extensive study of parenting styles and academic achievement was conducted by Dornbusch, Ritter, Leiderman, Roberts, and Fraleigh (1987). They found that significant and very consistent relationships existed between parenting styles and student grades. A questionnaire was distributed to 7,836 students attending six high schools in the San Francisco Bay area. About 88% of the total enrollment responded. Questions covered student background, self-reported grades, perceptions of parent attitudes and behavior, and family communication patterns. Three parenting styles (authoritarian, permissive, and authoritative) were identified and correlated with student grades, parent education levels, ethnicity, and family structure.

Across all ethnic groups, education levels, and family structures, the researchers consistently found that authoritarian parenting was associated with the lowest grades, permissive parenting with the next lowest, and authoritative with the highest grades (mean grade point average of 3.2). Inconsistent parenting—switching from one style to the other—was found to be strongly associated with low grades. These researchers concluded that parenting style is a more powerful predictor of student achievement than parent education, ethnicity, or family structure.

A later study by the same researchers was conducted to examine the extent to which positive effects of authoritative parenting held across various ethnic groups, social classes, and family structures (Steinberg, Mounts, Lamborn, & Dornbusch, 1989). The sample consisted of 8,000 high school students from nine high schools in Wisconsin and California. Results were consistent with the previously cited research in that authoritative parenting was positively correlated with academic success. Furthermore, the study examined other social-psychological outcomes of parenting style and found authoritative parenting also to be positively correlated with greater adolescent self-reliance, less psychological distress, and less delinquent behavior.

Ginsburg and Bronstein (1993) in a study of fifth-grade students found overcontrolling parental styles, characterized by high parental surveillance of homework, punitive reactions to grades, and use of extrinsic rewards for achievement, to be correlated with lower academic performance and decreased motivation to learn. Conversely, the parent–child relationship experienced by successful students is more likely to be characterized by frequent dialogues between parents and children, strong parent encouragement of academic pursuits, clear and consistent limits for children, warm and nurturing interactions, and consistent monitoring of how time is used (Clark, 1983). Children of parents who set clear limits and expectations such that their children know what is expected of them, and who model behaviors that emphasize education, perform better in school (Williams, 1994). Moreover, such authoritative parenting styles are also associated with decreased substance abuse, fewer mental health problems, and fewer behavioral problems with adolescents, along with improved academic achievement (Cohen & Rice, 1997; Shek, 1997). Authoritative parenting includes a high degree of involvement, a high degree of monitoring, and a high degree of psychological autonomy granting (Lam, 1997).

Clark (1983) conducted in-depth case studies of 10 Black families living in Chicago public housing projects. Clark's findings indicated that in the high achievers' homes, regardless of whether the family had one or two parents, the parenting style was considered authoritative and characterized by frequent dialogues between parents and children, strong parent encouragement of academic pursuits, clear and consistent limits for children, warm and nurturing interactions, and consistent monitoring of how time is used. Clark concluded that the overall quality of a family's lifestyle, not marital status, educational level, income, or social surroundings, is what determines children's level of preparedness for competent school performance. Further, his results supported the previously cited research on parental involvement, noting that parents of high achievers also visited the school periodically, got acquainted with the teachers, and became involved in various school activities.

Several other studies have consistently found a positive relationship between authoritative parenting style and academic achievement. In a study of parenting style and achievement with eighth graders at two inner-city Midwestern communities, Lam (1997) obtained similar results. In her sample of 181 students, she found a significant positive relationship between authoritative parenting and academic achievement. Slicker (1998) found that authoritative parenting styles were correlated with better school adjustment among high school students. Johnson's (1997) study of kindergarten and first-grade students and Marjoribanks' (1996) study of elementary-age students both produced results supportive of the previous studies, indicating that parenting style was associated with academic achievement and social achievement.

Vandell and Posner (1998) studied parenting style effects on achievement and behavioral adjustment of elementary school students from low-income urban families. Firm, authoritative parenting was found to be associated with better academic performance, social behavior, and child responsibility both at home and in school. Parental harshness was correlated with lower academic achievement and increased behavior difficulties in the home and school. Furthermore, the strength of the correlations increased by grade level, suggesting that without intervention the problems developing in the early elementary years will escalate as the child progresses through the educational system. Cohen and Rice (1997) found similar results regarding authoritative parenting styles among adolescents. In a study of eighth- and ninth-grade students, they found adolescents' perceptions of parenting styles to be positively correlated with academic achievement. Additionally, they found adolescent tobacco and alcohol use to be correlated with higher permissive and authoritarian parenting styles and inversely correlated with authoritative parenting styles.

Fathers and Education

Researchers investigating children's adjustment issues have tended to focus primarily on mothers and children. School programs for parents have also traditionally been heavily dominated by mothers who are more likely than fathers to attend a school event (National Center for Education Statistics, 1997). Some researchers have estimated that at least 50% of all children today will spend at least some portion of their school years in a single-parent household (Furstenberg & Cherlin, 1991). The overwhelming majority of these children will live with their mothers as the custodial single parent. The tendency, therefore, is for schools to focus on mothers' school involvement rather than fathers'. However, although the research on the fathers' influences on children's adjustment is still somewhat limited and inconsistent in design, the importance of the father's role must be recognized and father involvement fostered.

Studies have typically found that fathers are more likely to be involved with their sons than with their daughters (Lamb, 1986; Marsiglio, 1991). Close father–son relationships appear to be correlated with the cognitive abilities of boys and the development of analytic skills (Radin, 1981). Thompson (1986) has also found that although fathers tend to spend less time with their children, the importance of fathers in children's development actually increases as children grow older. Although mothers play a stronger role in emotional support and companionship, fathers seem to be associated more with learning and achievement factors in children's lives. One plausible conclusion from the existing body of research is that maternal involvement is beneficial for the social and emotional adjustment of children to school but that paternal involvement may be most important for academic achievement (National Center for Educational Statistics, 1997).

Counselors working with children experiencing academic difficulties are well advised to attempt to involve fathers as well as mothers in their interventions. This may involve flexible scheduling of conferences and specific requests or calls to fathers to attend such conferences or counseling sessions. Further, school counselors need to take a proactive approach to encouraging paternal involvement in their children's education. Father-focused programs at the school and information on the importance of paternal involvement should be provided. Programs can be implemented to meet the unique needs of all types of fathers, including fathers in two-parent homes, single custodial parent fathers, and noncustodial fathers. Such programs should also take into consideration the cultural backgrounds of fathers and the role this may play in their approach to parenting.

Implications for Teacher Consultation

The importance of parenting style—that is, parent–child interaction patterns—in relation to academic and social-behavioral adjustment has implications for classroom climate and teaching style. Paulsen, Marchant, and Rothlisberg (1997) found that students' perceptions of parenting style in regard to high responsiveness, valuing achievement, involvement in school functions, and moderate parental demands were correlated with higher achievement. However, they also found that similar patterns in the teacher's relationship style with students had similar outcome effects. High teacher responsiveness, classroom structure, and positive school atmosphere were correlated with higher achievement. Further analyses revealed that students who perceived authoritative adult–child interaction styles at home and at school had the highest grades, perceptions of grade importance, and perceptions of their own competence. Students who perceived incongruent styles between home and school had lower achievement, with lowest achievement outcomes occurring with the combination of neglectful, disengaged parenting styles and authoritarian teaching styles.

Many studies have identified teacher–student relationship variables as important correlates of students' academic performance, learning motivation, and school attitudes (Chiu & Tulley, 1997; Pert & Campbell, 1999; Wentzel, 1997; Wilson, 1997). Students who view their teachers as empathic, warm, friendly, and as having a genuine concern for them as individuals appear to perform better academically, display more positive attitudes toward school, and engage in fewer problematic classroom behaviors (Aspy, Roebuck, & Aspy, 1984; Branwhite, 1988; Niebuhr & Niebuhr, 1999;Waxman, 1983; Weishen & Peng, 1993). School counselors need to be able to go beyond family counseling and apply a similar systemic intervention strategy in teacher consultation regarding student difficulties. Preventive in-service training programs in effective teacher–student relationship styles might also be provided for school staff as part of a comprehensive school counseling program. Such programs might include training in authoritative classroom management strategies and the development of a positive classroom climate as well as in effective parent conferencing skills and strategies for fostering home–school collaboration.

It is interesting to note that teachers are often specifically trained to use classroom behavior management models that are authoritarian in nature—and focused on behavioral compliance through the use of reward and punishment strategies. Such models are often taught to educators through both preservice and in-service training programs, despite the large body of research that contraindicates the use of such models because they adversely impact students' academic achievement, learning motivation, and social adjustment. It is highly probable that teachers and administrators, trained in such counterproductive approaches, will be likely to suggest similar strategies to parents when confronted with a child's school adjustment difficulty. Dornbusch et al. (1987), for example, found that parents, when dealing with a child's behavior problem, will tend to use more intensive strategies consistent with the parenting style already employed (i.e., more authoritarian, more permissive, more disengaged, or more authoritative), which serves to exacerbate problems for those employing authoritarian, permissive, or disengaged parenting styles.

Developing Family-Focused Counseling Programs in Schools

Given the overwhelming research evidence documenting the key role played by family dynamics in children's social and academic adjustment, school counselors and other professionals working with children's academic and social adjustment difficulties must be prepared to provide both preventive and direct counseling services to parents and families (Nicoll, 1984, 1992, 1994). Further, given the evidence documenting the effects of classroom climate, teacher–student interaction styles, and home–school collaboration on students' academic achievement, consulting and training services must also be provided for teachers and other school personnel in these areas.

Family-focused school counseling programs should strive to facilitate the development of congruent adult–child interaction styles in home and school that are based on the authoritative model, thereby creating a common vocabulary and shared understanding of children among the primary caregivers—parents and teachers. School counseling programs need to place greater emphasis on developing strategies for facilitating positive, effective parent involvement and home–school collaboration programs through parent education programs and the establishment of parent-teacher resource centers in the schools. In addition, school counseling programs need to place greater emphasis on providing direct brief family counseling and solution-focused parent conference interventions. Such programs will not only increase the effectiveness of the counseling interventions but also increase community support for the school and counseling program.

Family Counseling and Consultation

Family counseling and consulting services can be delivered directly through the schools (Nicoll, 1992, 1994). For example, referrals for either academic or psychosocial adjustment concerns might include an assessment of possible family functioning factors in the etiology and maintenance of the problem behavior. Shek (1997), for example, found that adolescents' (i.e., children 12 to 16 years of age) perceptions of family functioning level were strongly correlated with mental health problems, problematic behaviors, and poorer academic achievement. Counselors, therefore, need to work directly with the family as well as the student in their assessment and intervention strategies.

Given the large caseloads of counselors working in schools and the complexity of their tasks and responsibilities, brief family counseling and consultation intervention models seem particularly well suited to the educational setting (Nicoll, 1992). Such an approach allows both parents and teachers to become involved collaboratively in resolving student learning and behavioral difficulties in partnership with the counselor and student. Parents and teachers can be assisted in recognizing the interactional patterns within the family system, as well as the classroom system, that may be maintaining the presenting problem. Counselors are then in a position to develop interventions that will effectively alter the dysfunctional adult–child or parent–child–school interaction patterns.

Parent-Teacher Resource Centers

The creation of parent–teacher resource centers is another possible component of a comprehensive family-based program that provides preventive and early intervention services. Such centers have been established in schools to provide information and training on raising and educating children. By educating both parents and teachers regarding family dynamics and achievement and effective home and classroom child-rearing practices, a congruent and effective style of parenting and teaching can be established to facilitate improved social and academic adjustment. Norwood, Atkinson, and Tellez (1997), for example, found positive effects on academic achievement from implementing a school-based parent education program targeted at an at-risk school population. The parent education program focused on developing both positive behavior management strategies and practical methods for increasing parent involvement in their children's education. Similarly, Becher (1984) found that parent education programs, particularly with low-income parents, are effective in improving children's language skills, test performance, and school behavior.

Formal parent education programs consistent with the authoritative parenting model, such as Systematic Training in Effective Parenting (STEP) (Dinkmeyer, McKay, & Dinkmeyer, 1997) or Active Parenting (Popkin, 1983), can be offered through the parent-teacher resource center to train parents in effective child-rearing practices. Such centers can also serve as places where parents may obtain information on community resources and effective strategies for parental involvement in education at home. Programs and activities that strengthen and empower families have also been offered through these centers, such as establishing baby-sitting cooperatives, sharing used books and educational materials, and organizing family activities, such as field trips and science activity nights. Some centers have also implemented open-forum family counseling sessions (Christensen & Schramski, 1983) as an effective means of providing ongoing supportive family counseling and parent education services while also fostering a sense of community, understanding, and mutual support among parents and teachers.

Similarly, formal in-service professional development programs for teachers can be established through the parent-teacher resource center. Such training should focus on authoritative classroom behavior management and student motivation strategies. Teachers could learn practical strategies for creating positive classroom and school climates. Programs such as Cooperative Discipline (Albert, 1996) or Positive Discipline in the Classroom (Nelson, Lott, & Glenn, 1993) are designed to train teachers in authoritative teaching styles.

By training both parents and teachers to work congruently with an authoritative approach to interacting with children and adolescents at home and school, more positive and effective child-rearing environments can be created, leading to increased academic achievement, fewer special education placements, and improved social-emotional adjustment. A parent-teacher resource center can also implement programs that facilitate home–school collaboration and parental involvement, both of which are associated with improved academic success and social adjustment.

Conclusion

Counseling interventions for child and adolescent difficulties are far more effective when directed at altering interaction patterns between the child and the significant adults in his or her life—parents and teachers. Further, the research knowledge base on family dynamics and achievement overwhelmingly advocates for implementing programs designed to facilitate the development of adult–child interaction styles consistent with the authoritative model—the adult–child interaction style most highly correlated with academic achievement and positive psychosocial development. Parent education and parent–teacher resource centers combined with a brief family counseling consultation approach to interventions for school problems appear to offer ideal strategies for increasing the visibility and effectiveness of counseling in educational settings while simultaneously providing optimal services to the school and community.

References

Albert, L. (1996). *Cooperative discipline.* Circle Pines, MN: American Guidance Services.

Aspy, D. N., Roebuck, F. N., & Aspy, C. B. (1984). Tomorrow's resources are in today's classroom. *Personnel Guidance Journal, 62,* 455–459.

Baker, A.J.L., & Soden, L. M. (1998). *The challenges of parent involvement research.* New York: ERIC Clearinghouse on Urban Education. (ERIC Document Reproduction Service No. ED419030)

Baumrind, D. (1967). Effects of authoritative parental control on child behavior. *Child Development, 37,* 887–907.

Baumrind, D. (1975). The contributions of the family to the development of competence in children. *Schizophrenia Bulletin, 14,* 12–37.

Becher, R. M. (1984). *Parent involvement: A review of research and principles of successful practice.* Washington, DC: National Institute of Education. (ERIC Document Reproduction Service No. ED247032)

Benson, C. S., Buckley, S., & Medrich, E. A. (1980). Families as educators: Time use contributions to school achievement. In J. Guthrie (Ed.), *School finance policies and practices: The 1980s: A decade of conflict* (pp.169–204). Cambridge, MA: Ballinger.

Bloom, B. S. (1985). *Developing talent in young people.* New York: Ballantine.

Branwhite, T. (1988). The PASS survey: School-based preferences of 500+ adolescent consumers. *Educational Studies, 14,* 165–176.

Caplan, N., Choy, M. H., & Whitmore, J. K. (1992, February). Indochinese refugee families and academic achievement. *Scientific American,* 36–42.

Chiu L. H., & Tulley, M. (1997). Student preferences of teacher discipline styles. *Journal of Instructional Psychology, 24*(3), 168–175.

Christensen, O. C., & Schramski, T. (1983). *Adlerian family counseling.* Minneapolis, MN: Educational Media.

Clark, R. M. (1983). *Family life and school achievement: Why poor Black children succeed or fail.* Chicago: University of Chicago Press.

Clark, R. M. (1993). Homework-focused parenting practices that positively affect student achievement. In N. F. Chavkin (Ed.), *Families and schools in a pluralistic society* (pp. 85–105). Albany: State University of New York Press.

Clarke, J. S. (1993). *Strategies addressing discrepancies in educational and behavioral priorities and expectations between staff and middle-*

class K-5 parents. Fort Lauderdale, FL: Nova University, Department of Education.

Cohen, D. A., & Rice, J. (1997). Parenting styles, adolescent substance use, and academic achievement. *Journal of Drug Education, 27*(2), 199–211.

Cummings, C., & Haggerty, K. P. (1997, May). Raising healthy children. *Educational Leadership, 54*(8), 28–30.

Dahir, C., Sheldon, C., & Valiga, M. (1998). *Vision into action: Implementing the National Standards for School Counseling Programs.* Alexandria, VA: American Counseling Association.

Darling, N. (1999). *Parenting style and its correlates.* Washington, DC: Office of Educational Research and Improvement. (ERIC Document Reproduction Service No. ED427896)

Dauber, S., & Epstein, J. (1993). Parent attitudes and practices of involvement in inner-city elementary and middle schools. In N. F. Chavkin (Ed.), *Families and schools in a pluralistic society* (pp. 53–71). Albany: State University of New York Press.

Deslandes, R., Royer, E., & Turcotte, D. (1997). School achievement at the secondary level: Influence of parenting style and parent involvement in schooling. *McGill Journal of Education, 32,* 191–207.

Dinkmeyer, D., McKay, G. D., & Dinkmeyer, D. (1997). *Systematic training for effective parenting.* Circle Pines, MN: American Guidance Services.

Dornbusch, S., Ritter, P., Leiderman, P. H., Roberts, D. F., & Fraleigh, M. (1987). The relation of parenting style to adolescent school performance. *Child Development, 58,* 1244–1257.

Eccles, J. S., & Harold, R. D. (1996). Family involvement in children and adolescents' schooling. In A. Booth & J. F. Dunn (Eds.), *Family-school links: How do they affect educational outcomes?* (pp. 3–34). Mahwah, NJ: Lawrence Erlbaum.

Epstein, J. L. (1990). School and family connections: Theory, research, and implications for integrating sociologies of education and family. *Marriage and Family Review, 15,* 99–126.

Ferguson, R. F. (1991). Paying for public education: New evidence of how and why money matters. *Harvard Journal on Legislation, 28,* 465–498.

Furstenberg, F. F., & Cherlin, A. J. (1991). *Divided families: What happens to children when parents part.* Cambridge, MA: Harvard University Press.

Garcia, D. C. (1990). *Creating parental involvement: A manual for school children and parents interacting program.* Miami: Florida International University, School of Education.

Ginsburg, G. S., & Bronstein, P. (1993). Family factors related to children's intrinsic/extrinsic motivational orientation and academic performance. *Child Development, 64*(5), 1461–1474.

Good, T. L., & Brophy, J. E. (1986). School effects. In M. C. Wittrock (Ed.), *The handbook of research on teaching* (3rd ed., pp. 570–604). New York: Macmillan.

Gysbers, N. C., & Henderson, P. (1988). *Developing and managing your school guidance program.* Alexandria, VA: American Association for Counseling and Development.

Henderson, A. T., & Berla, N. (1995). *A new generation of evidence: The family is critical to student achievement.* Washington, DC: Center for Law and Education.

Hickman, C. W., Greenwood, G., & Miller, M. D. (1995). High school parent involvement: Relationships with achievement, grade level, SES and gender. *Journal of Research and Development in Education, 28*(3), 125–134.

Irvine, D. J. (1979). *Parent involvement affects children's cognitive growth.* Albany: University of the State of New York, State Education Department, Division of Research. (ERIC Document Reproduction Service No. ED176893)

Johnson, V.J.K. (1997, April). *Family level processes in children's adaptation to school.* Paper presented at the Biennial Meeting of the Society for Research in Child Development, Washington, DC. (ERIC Document Reproduction Service No. ED408025)

Lam, S. F. (1997). *How the family influences children's academic achievement.* Hamden, CT: Garland.

Lamb, M. E. (1986). *The father's role: Applied perspectives.* New York: Wiley.

Marjoribanks, K. (1996). Family socialization and children's school outcomes: An investigation of a parenting model. *Educational Studies, 22*(1), 3–11.

Maccoby, E., & Martin, J. (1983). Socialization in the context of the family: Parent–child interaction. In P. H. Mussen (Series Ed.) & E. M. Hetherington (Vol. Ed.), *Handbook of child psychology: Vol. 4. Socialization, personality, and social development* (4th ed., pp. 1–101). New York: Wiley.

Marsiglio, W. (1991). Paternal engagement activities with minor children. *Journal of Marriage and the Family, 53*(4), 973–986.

Milner, E. (1951). A study of the relationship between reading readiness in grade one school children and patterns of parent–child interactions. *Child Development, 22*(2), 95–112.

Moos, R. H. (1974). *Family environment scale.* Palo Alto, CA: Consulting Psychologists Press.

Myrick, R. D. (1993). *Developmental guidance and counseling: A practical approach* (2nd ed.). Minneapolis, MN: Educational Media.

National Center for Education Statistics. (1997). *Fathers' involvement in their children's schools.* Washington, DC: U.S. Department of Education Office of Educational Research and Improvement. (NCES 98-091R)

National Educational Goals Panel. (1994). *The national education goals report: Building a nation of learners.* Washington, DC: U.S. Government Printing Office.

Nelson, J., Lott, L., & Glenn, H. S. (1993). *Positive discipline in the classroom.* Rocklin, CA: Prima.

Nicoll, W. G. (1984). School counselors as family counselors: A rationale and training model. *The School Counselor, 31*(3), 279–284.

Nicoll, W. G. (1991). Working effectively with parents and families: Developing the school counselor's skills. In D. R. Coy (Ed.), *ASCA professional development in-service workshop outlines*. Alexandria, VA: American School Counselor Association.

Nicoll, W. G. (1992). A family counseling/consultation model for school counselors. *The School Counselor, 39*(5), 351–361.

Nicoll, W. G. (1994). A response to school-based collaboration with families. *The Family Journal: Counseling and therapy for couples and families, 2*(4), 301–312.

Niebuhr, K. E., & Niebuhr, R. E. (1999). An empirical study of student relationships and academic achievement. *Education, 119*(4), 679.

Nord, C. W. (1998). *Factors associated with fathers' and mothers' involvement in their children's schools*. Washington, DC: National Center for Education Statistics. (ERIC Document Reproduction Service No. ED417872)

Norwood, P., Atkinson, S., & Tellez, K. (1997). Contextualizing parent education programs in urban schools: The impact on minority parents and students. *Urban Education, 32*, 411–432.

Paulson, S. E., Marchant, G. J., & Rothlisberg, B. A. (1997). Early adolescents' perceptions of patterns of parenting, teaching, and school atmosphere: Implications for achievement. *Journal of Early Adolescence, 18*, 5–12.

Pert, N. A., & Campbell, F. A. (1999). At-risk students' perceptions of teacher effectiveness. *Journal for a Just and Caring Education, 5*(3), 269–284.

Popkin, M. H. (1983). *Active parenting*. Atlanta, GA: Active Parenting.

Radin, N. (1981). The role of the father in cognitive, academic, and intellectual development. In M. E. Lamb (Ed.), *The role of the father in child development* (pp. 379–427). New York: Wiley.

Resnick, M. D., Bearman, P. S., Blum, R. W., Bauman, K. E., Harris, K. M., Jones, J., et al. (1997). Protecting adolescents from harm: Findings from the national longitudinal study on adolescent health. *Journal of the American Medical Association, 278*(10), 823–832.

Shek, D. (1997). The relation of family functioning to adolescent psychological well-being, school adjustment, and problem behavior. *Journal of Genetic Psychology, 158*, 467–480.

Slicker, E. K. (1998). Relationship of parenting style to behavioral adjustment in graduating high school seniors. *Journal of Youth and Adolescence, 27*(3), 345–373.

Steinberg, L., Mounts, N. S., Lamborn, S. D., & Dornbusch, S. (1989, April). *Authoritative parenting and adolescent adjustment across varied ecological niches*. Paper presented at the biennial meeting of the Society for Research in Child Development, Kansas City, MO.

Swap, S. M. (1993). *Developing home-school partnerships: From concepts to practice*. New York: Teachers College Press, Columbia University.

Thompson, R. A. (1986). Fathers and the child's best interests: Judicial decision making in custody disputes. In M. E. Lamb (Ed.), *The father's role: Applied perspectives.* New York: Wiley.

Vaden-Kiernan, N., & Davies, B. (1993). *Parent involvement.* Unpublished manuscript.

Vandell, D., & Posner, J. (1998). Harsh, firm, and permissive parenting in low-income families: Relations to children's academic achievement and behavioral adjustment. *Journal of Family Issues, 19,* 483–507.

Walz, G. R. (1988). *Building strong school counseling programs.* Alexandria, VA: American Association for Counseling and Development.

Waxman, H. C. (1983). Effect of teachers' empathy on students' motivation. *Psychological Reports, 53,* 489–490.

Weishen, N., & Peng, L. (1993). Variables predicting students' problem behaviors. *Journal of Educational Research, 87,* 5–17.

Wentzel, K. R. (1997). Student motivation in middle school: The role of perceived pedagogical caring. *Journal of Educational Psychology, 89*(3), 411–419.

White-Clark, R., & Decker, L. E. (1996). *The "hard-to-reach" parent: Old challenges, new insights.* Fairfax, VA: National Community Education Association.

Williams, W. A. (1994, October). *Test scores, school performance, and parenting issues: Assuring academic achievement. The connection between family life and school achievement: Given a supportive family, Black children can succeed.* Paper presented at the meeting of the National Conference of the Black Child Development Institute, Seattle, WA. (ERIC Document Reproduction Service No. ED376264)

Wilson, P. (1997). Key factors in the performance and achievement of minority students at the University of Alaska, Fairbanks. *American Indian Quarterly, 21*(3), 535–544.

Zill, N., & Nord, C. W. (1994). *Running in place: How American families are faring in a changing economy and an individualistic society.* Washington, DC: Child Trends.

■ ■ ■

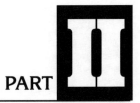

PART **II**

SCHOOL
COUNSELING
TECHNIQUES

3

Creating Solution-Focused Families: Tools for School Counselors

Bobbie Birdsall, PhD

Copernicus came along and made a startling reversal: He put the sun in the center of the universe, rather than the earth. His declaration caused profound shock. The earth was not the epitome of creation; it was a planet like all other planets. The successful challenge to the entire system of ancient authority required a complete change in the philosophical conception of the universe (Turnbull & Summers, p.12, as cited in Fuller & Olsen, 1998). Changing beliefs and values from an earth-centered universe to a sun-centered universe took extraordinary effort and sustained levels of confidence in this new way of viewing the universe. Similarly, family systems counseling seeks to place the child in his or her rightful place within the family, rather than as the center of family functioning. This "revolutionary" thinking of people within the larger context of a family constellation requires consistent attention to the family system and the act of viewing individuals as responding to natural forces and relational ties, rather than simply looking at the person in isolation.

This chapter discusses further the conceptual shift of individual counseling to systems counseling, but specifically discusses a brief solution-focused model. This brief approach responds to a new era of mental health reform, in which insurance companies offer a limited number of mental health sessions. If sessions are limited to 10 to 20 per year, counselors need to tailor treatment planning to this time frame. A brief focused intervention, with solution finding as a goal, is well suited for a school setting. This process of intervening in a family system in a school setting from a brief solution-focused approach is detailed. Pitfalls of this approach are discussed and a case study is offered. An appendix lists Web sites and a print resource helpful in brief and family-related counseling.

A Family Systems Conceptual Framework

A paradigm shift has been evolving in counseling for more than 30 years. With the advent of systems theory and family therapy, the focus has turned away from the individual and has turned to social networks (Amatea, 1989; Hinkle, 1993; Littrell, Malia, & Vanderwood, 1995). Family systems theory views the family as a social system wherein all members have an impact on each other, and the basic premise is that the individual members of a family are so interrelated that any experience or problem affecting one member will affect all (Carter & McGoldrick, 1980). Carter and Sweeney (1994) noted that long before children set foot in a classroom, their families have taught them attitudes and expectations regarding education. When children have problems at home, the problems cannot help but enter the classroom. Steinberg (1996) reported that research findings of a study of 20,000 teenagers and their families suggest that the dismal state of student achievement in America is caused more by the conditions of students' lives outside of school than the events that take place within school walls.

When a child has a problem, it often can be connected to the family. Interventions that involve only the child are less effective in improving academic success (Evans & Carter, 1997). Family systems theory is a viable approach to conceptualizing behavior and problems within the context of the family, rather than within a certain individual's behavior. For instance, a child may be sad and withdrawn at school, often not completing assignments. This problem may be in response to his or her parents' divorce. Thus, it is best to help solve the problem by including the school and family in formulating a solution (Hinkle, 1993).

As a result of this thinking, counseling in the schools has begun a shift to viewing the student as part of a larger unit—his or her family. School counselors are "learning to change their perception of school counseling from traditional student-focused problems to more systemic issues found in families and the system of schools and families working together" (Cowie & Quinn, 1997, p. 57). To incorporate a family-centered philosophy, a paradigm shift must occur. What must now accompany the school counselor's perspective of the problem—to be reflective of a system problem—is the creation of a systemic solution. Contributing to each child's education is a strong partnership between the school and family. Intervention on the part of school counselors must move away from being child or student focused to being family focused (Fuller & Olsen, 1998).

School-Based Family Counseling

School counselors have a unique position as insiders within a school system. Family counseling or school-based counseling models are being developed using this unique position to intervene effectively with various behavior problems in the school and to increase students' academic success (Kraus, 1998). Counselors seldom get involved in the life of a student without considering the continuous influence of the family as the primary social system (Lewis, 1996). "Many approaches to family counseling exist; however, a brief format seems to fit the school counseling environment the best" (Hinkle, 1993, p. 253). One study has suggested that the brief counseling format is best suited to children's emotional regulation and school-related issues (Lee, 1997). Murphy (1994) pointed out that advantages for school counselors using the solution-focused model include (a) an increase of cooperative relationships among school staff, parents, and students; (b) more time efficiency; and (c) a more realistic approach for a school setting than the often vague approaches. The traditional model of school counseling assumed that counselors had generous amounts of time to work with students. The reality is that time is often limited because of the disproportionate counselor-student ratio (Amatea, 1989) as well as competing administrative tasks. A more realistic, time-limited family counseling model integrates family systems theory with solution-focused family counseling in the school setting.

By incorporating family counseling in the school setting, parents and teachers can be assisted in recognizing the interaction patterns and structures of the family system, as well as of the classroom system and total school environment, that have developed around a student's particular problem and may now serve to maintain or eliminate the difficulty (Walsh & Williams, 1997). Schools can begin by creating short-term counseling for students and their families.

A typical child-study team meeting may proceed like this: The teacher brings the student's problem to the team. The school psychologist may be asked to do psychological testing or to comment on previously administered standardized test scores in the student's cumulative file. The school counselor is asked to provide background regarding the factors influencing the student's problem, such as family issues. The general result is that the school psychologist labels the child, and the school counselor is asked to meet with the parents, often concluding, "What can you do? Just look at the parents!" The label almost guarantees failure to help the student. After labeling, no one seems to know what to do to find a solution.

For years, school counselors have struggled with trying to help students without working with parents. In situations in which they have been able to work with the parents, the approach often has been based on behavioral management procedures and the attitude that the problem should be the focus of counseling. In fact, parents and teachers often expect school counselors to fix the problem. The solution-focused model shifts the emphasis from unacceptable behaviors to locating exceptions when the problem behavior does not occur.

In the traditional model, the school counselor uses two strategies in dealing with problems. The first is to arrange for parent-teacher conferences limited by the time structure of the school day. If the problem is chronic or severe, this contact may not be adequate. If the first strategy fails to bring about desired change, the second strategy is to refer the child to the child-study team that may in turn refer the child to an outside professional counselor. Because restructuring is the current mode of educational reform, it is appropriate to restructure the school counseling model by recognizing the family as a resource and working to empower parents and children through counseling (Kraus, 1998).

When considering integrating family systems theory into the schools, using the solution-focused family counseling model makes sense in two important ways: The family is viewed as critical to student success, and solutions, not problems, become the focus. Families are given hope that they can be successful in helping their children and their entire family system.

School counselors are becoming familiar with brief counseling interventions because they are finding that the interventions make sense in the school setting. A study reported by Evans and Carter (1997) indicated that a brief school-based model makes an impact on the attendance, academic achievement, and classroom behavior of children referred for emotional and behavioral problems. School counselors work under time constraints and find that brief interventions are dictated. Counselors have remedial, preventive, and crisis response roles in addition to counseling, consultation, and coordinating roles. They often find themselves limited in how they are able to serve students best. Using brief counseling interventions with families offers a new paradigm for helping students in a school-based family counseling model.

Going back to the child-study team scenario: When teachers, counselors, and staff begin to view the child through a positive lens and look for a time when the child is behaving in the appropriate manner, the paradigm begins to shift, and a solution-focused school atmosphere begins to emerge. When school personnel begin to acknowledge that (a) families know certain aspects of their children better than anyone else, (b) families have the greatest vested interest in seeing their children learn, and (c) the family is likely to be the only group of adults involved with a child's educational program throughout his or her entire school career (Fuller & Olsen, 1998), school-based family counseling is viewed in a positive light. In addition, school-based family counseling works equally effectively with boys and girls, different age groups, and families from diverse backgrounds and with differences in demographic characteristics (Lee, 1997).

Tools for School Counselors

Not all school counselors have received training in brief counseling interventions with families or a school-based counseling model. Knowledge about the solution-focused family counseling model, family systems theory, and family dynamics used in the structural approach will help counselors incorporate family counseling in the school setting. A basic assumption of the brief model is less interest in the past history of problems and more interest in small successes through behavior change. At least two important skills are necessary to do school-based family counseling: assessing the family's ability to change and defining which systems (parent, school, community) are involved in the problematic behavior (Kraus, 1998).

Evaluating Family Functioning

It is important for the school counselor to evaluate the level of each family's functioning before determining if the solution-focused counseling model will be effective. A primary skill for counselors doing brief family counseling is assessing the family's capacity for change. Healthy families typically exhibit clear communication, mutual respect, a loving attitude, role flexibility, individuation of members, and security (Kraus, 1998). Assessment should include all family members' understanding of the problem, resources and strengths of the family, and what interventions the family has tried (Hinkle, 1993). Understanding family dynamics from the structural approach will give information for this evaluation. Family dynamics and terminology, such as structure, subsystems, enmeshment, disengagement, rules, cohesiveness, and boundaries, will be useful in identifying functionality (Goldenberg & Goldenberg, 2000). The checklist in Figure 3.1 can be used for evaluating the readiness of each family for the solution-focused counseling model. It is important to discover who is included in the definition of the family. Families take many forms and many different compositions; being more inclusive of members (even though not all members are present) is typically more helpful in discovering functionality.

FIGURE 3.1
Checklist for Evaluating Family Functionality

	Yes/No
TIME FRAME OF PROBLEMATIC BEHAVIOR	
• Is the misbehavior of a relatively short history?	____
• Is there an identifiable psychosocial stressor?	____
FAMILY STRUCTURE	
• Are boundaries between family members clearly defined and permeable?	____
• Is the hierarchy of parental authority stable and effective?	____
• Is communication between family members relatively free and spontaneous?	____
PROBLEM-SOLVING SKILLS	
• Is the family able to agree on defining the problematic behavior and on possible solutions?	____
• Does the family follow through on agreed-upon tasks?	____

From *Family Counseling in School Settings* (p. 51), by W. M. Walsh and N. J. Giblin, 1988, Springfield, IL: Charles C Thomas. Copyright 1988 by W. M. Walsh. Reprinted with permission.

If most answers are "yes" on this checklist, solution-focused family counseling can be effective. The school counselor will need to have an initial interview with the family to determine the factors listed on the checklist. The counselor can then make a recommendation to the family as to whether school-based family counseling could be effective or whether it will be more appropriate to make an outside referral.

Family Developmental Stages

School counselors are often knowledgeable about developmental stages for students. "Counselors can play a critical role in sharing developmental information about children and adolescents with adults. This information can help parents and teachers better understand the young people in their lives and establish appropriate expectations for them" (Paisley & Benshoff, 1996, p. 166).

It is equally important for school counselors to have an understanding of family developmental stages as they counsel families. Healthy families undergo developmental change as well as dysfunctional families, and this normal change and growth may produce conflict in the family (Kraus, 1998). The transitions between stages are often characterized by stress, chaos, and conflict; for example, a child entering kindergarten for the first time or a parent returning to work when the children are a certain age can add another major element of conflict to family dynamics. Stages of the family life cycle for intact families with young children are as follows: the family with young children, and the family with adolescents. Families with young children must accept new members into the system and accomplish the following tasks: (a) adjust the marital system to make space for the child or children, (b) take on parenting roles, and (c) realign relationships with the extended family to include parenting and grandparenting roles. Families with adolescents must increase the flexibility of family boundaries to include children's independence and accomplish these tasks: (a) shift parent–child relationships to permit adolescents to move in and out of the system, (b) refocus in midlife marital and career issues, and (c) begin the shift toward concerns for the older generation (Carter & McGoldrick, 1980).

Family Genogram

Gathering information about the family can be accomplished through a family genogram (see Figure 3.2). In essence, the genogram is a schematic family tree including at least three generations. It details information on a chart regarding family marriages, divorces, deaths, medical history, occupational information, and crises. The school counselor and the family can begin to see patterns of family interactions and influences that previous family members may have had on current interactions.

Males are denoted by squares and females by circles. Years of birth are noted below the square or circle, or current ages are stated inside the circle or square. Horizontal lines indicate marriages (with the year of marriage, separation, or divorce denoted on the line), and vertical lines connect generations. Siblings are drawn from left to right in order of their birth. Drawing a genogram allows the counselor to get a visual description of a family and can often prompt spontaneous memories or recollections of emotional relatedness in family members.

Figure 3.2 shows the father (age 54) married three times, divorced three times. With his third wife, he has two children. William, currently age 10, is the second child of this union; he has a sister 10 years his senior. The mother (age 43) is remarried. The mother is the last child in a family of five. Notice that the career and educational pursuits of many relatives are noted.

Family counselors suggest that academic achievement patterns can be discerned through level of educational attainment information as well as questions regarding attitudes toward academic achievement. Was academic achievement encouraged, discouraged, or controlled? What were the rules or secrets regarding success (Walsh & Williams, 1997)? This information may help the family develop greater understanding and perhaps empathy for family dynamics over the generations and perhaps make new decisions regarding their current desires and attitudes toward academic achievement and success. This is searching for solutions, looking at family strengths through generations.

Solution-Focused Family Counseling

To implement solution-focused family counseling, it is essential to adopt the attitudes and principles that facilitate this model. The following attitudes and principles are salient:

- Keep a view towards family strengths, resources, and what's possible at the time. Focus on the present and the positive.
- Focus on goals, solutions, exceptions, and future visions to facilitate family change.

FIGURE 3.2
Genogram for William Nelson, Age 10

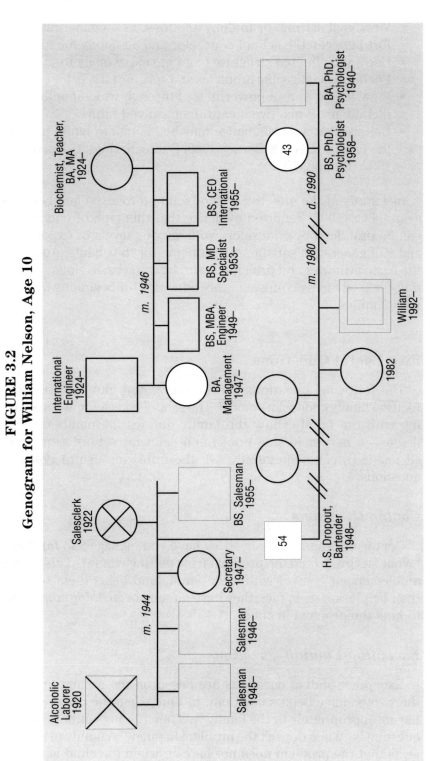

- View goal setting, or finding solutions, as a collaborative effort between the school counselor and all family members.
- Use a time-limited structure to create expectancy for change.
- Focus on manageable problems and specific targets for change.
- View language as a powerful tool through which families are invited into a positive and problem-solved future.
- Believe that a small change may be enough to ignite hope in the family. (Beck & Emery, 1985; Budman, Hoyt, & Friedman, 1992; Talmon, 1990)

In a study of the effectiveness of solution-focused family counseling, Lee (1997) reported evidence that this type of counseling can be practiced by counselors with varying levels of experience and still generate a satisfactory outcome for the clients. Adopting the basic attitudes and principles, and learning basic skills in solution-focused family counseling, are adequate for beginning to work with families.

Five Useful Questions

The following questions can be integrated into the solution-focused family counseling model. The school counselor, when meeting with the family (how the family defines its membership is discussed earlier in this book) and relevant school personnel (if needed), can sequentially ask the following useful types of questions.

Coping Questions

Coping questions include "How have you managed so far?" and "What has prevented the problem from getting worse?" This places an element of control within the family and helps them reframe their helplessness. In fact, they have already been doing something to hold the problem in check.

Exception-Finding Questions

Exception-finding questions are based on the assumption that there must have been some point in time when the child was behaving appropriately or the family was functioning better. A typical question is "When doesn't the problem happen?" A family often suggests that the problem does not happen when the child is asleep!

The counselor needs to explore exceptional times further, perhaps using prompts such as "Is there any time of the day that is better?" or "Is there a certain place where the behavior does not occur?" or even "Are there people who never see this behavior?" Find out what makes those circumstances unique.

Miracle Question

This question is "If a miracle happened and the problem were solved, what would you be doing differently or what would the family be doing differently?" The focus is on specific behaviors that family members would be engaged in that would let others in the family know that they were working on the solution.

Scaling Question

An example of a scaling question is "On a scale of 1 to 10, 1 being the problem is totally in control of the family and 10 being the family is in control of the problem, where is each family member today?" Different perceptions of the problem by individual family members can be very useful for processing the family dynamics. The follow-up question to the scaling question is "Where would family members like to be tomorrow or next week?" Then ask, "What one thing can the family do to increase control just a small amount?"

Task Development Question

The task development question follows the scaling question: "Based on the successes that family members have described today regarding this problem, what is one small goal the family can set to encourage this new behavior?"

Combining the Tools

In the solution-focused family counseling model, the counselor works with either the whole family or with any member who is motivated to come to counseling and assumes that a small change in one part of the family system will lead to changes in other parts. The following example illustrates how the school counselor can combine family systems theory, structural family therapy concepts, family developmental stages, genograms, and solution-focused family counseling.

William's fifth grade teacher notices that William is constantly disrupting the classroom, interrupts the teacher, is off-task, and has difficulty making friends in the classroom. She brings this to the attention of the school counselor, Ms. Vaughan, who observes these behaviors firsthand in the classroom. Ms. Vaughan calls William's parents, the Nelsons, to set up a family counseling appointment in her office. She explains to the parents that her belief is that the student can become more successful in the classroom with the help of the whole family.

When the family arrives, Ms. Vaughan begins by acknowledging the family's presence and affirming the importance of their attendance. She then describes the behavior that she and the teacher noticed and asks each family member for input regarding this behavior. She proceeds by asking the family how they operate in terms of rules, boundaries, subsystems, and so on.

Next, she describes the family's life-cycle stage at this point in time for the Nelson family as well as the developmental stage for William. She then invites the family to create a family genogram (Figure 3.2). The Nelsons notice a pattern of working outside the home and not having much time with the children. This was also a pattern with the grandparents on both sides. There is also a clear pattern of academic success on the maternal side. A pattern of multiple marriages also emerges on the side of William's biological father. The counselor may be prompted to ask about visitation for William and provide useful separation and reentry skills for the family to exercise.

The Five Useful Questions are asked next to implement solution-focused family counseling. The family agrees that to help William, the entire family needs to be doing something differently. They describe a future vision of spending more family time together and paying more attention to William's needs. They will specifically spend Saturday afternoon playing tennis or swimming as a family. In addition, each parent will spend 30 minutes with William each school day, playing and finishing schoolwork. William's future vision is that he will be doing his work and not interrupting his teacher. He describes a time in last year's class when he enjoyed doing the work and was able to pay attention. The school counselor asks permission to contact the biological father to help him to reinforce these same goals.

Each family member is asked the scaling question, and the consensus is the scale is at a 4, with the problem being in control. The family agrees that to move the scale to a 5 this week, they will begin with one parent spending 30 minutes each evening with William and the entire family going swimming on Saturday. William agrees that he will not interrupt his teacher this week.

At the end of the session, the family is given encouragement and hope that they can make things better. They leave with a concrete strategy that enables them to feel they can control the problem. The family is then invited for a follow-up session and to attend the parent education classes that the school counselor offers.

Other Family Interventions

To incorporate a family-centered philosophy in the schools, family-focused interventions should include a comprehensive program of services, including parent-education activities and parent support groups as well as school-based family counseling (Schmidt, 1996). Traditional parent education classes have relied on providing information to enhance the overall effectiveness of parents and to help them develop the skills that will support their child's success and achievement.

Parent education groups using the brief therapy model have been developed as an alternative to more traditional models of intervention for the parents of adolescents with such problems as substance abuse (Selekman, 1991). These groups are designed to teach parents hands-on parenting skills and assist them in becoming aware of their own parental and family strengths and resources. The main emphasis is on what is working for the parents, rather than what the parents are doing wrong with their children.

School counselors can play a valuable role in assisting parents by creating social-emotional support systems in the schools. They can help organize support groups in which individual parents can receive help from a group of parents who share common interests and concerns (Fuller & Olsen, 1998). Group meetings can also allow parents to become more aware of specific problems that affect their children and prevention techniques (Evans & Carter, 1997).

Pitfalls of Solution-Focused Family Counseling

Solution-focused family counseling is a viable alternative for students with developmental concerns, (e.g., academic success issues, peer and parent conflicts, and stress management) and for students who want a brief number of sessions with concrete interventions (Littrell et al., 1995). Depending on the school system, there may be some pitfalls to the use of the solution-focused family counseling model. One is that a school counselor's flexibility in managing a family case within the school system can be limited by school district policy. For example, many schools require parent conferences with a school principal following suspension. In some cases parents react negatively to the administrator; thus, the counselor may not have the opportunity to create a partnership between family and school. Furthermore, as school employees, school counselors risk not having the choice about accepting a family for counseling

(Kral, 1990). Some families may not be appropriate for the counselor's training and expertise, or the parents may be resistant to commit to counseling.

Families may perceive a conflict of interest between helping the child and helping the family. Families may not understand the connection between family factors and a child's level of academic functioning (Evans & Carter, 1997). Resistance to the idea of seeking help with the counselor may develop if this occurs.

The school counselor must determine if a behavior problem or a student concern is valid and then provide the treatment for the child, if the school is structured around a family-focused paradigm. This expectation may deter the possibility of making outside referrals and may interfere with time constraints for the counselor. Also, family relationship issues are likely to be complex and may require in-depth therapy. Ethically, school counselors should not hesitate to refer families who require therapy that is beyond their expertise.

Because school counselors work under time constraints, time given to counseling families may affect time given to other counseling roles. School administrators and teachers must be made aware of the rationale behind working with students and families. The student–school–family interaction must be explained in detail, whether through in-service programs or orientation meetings at the beginning of the school year. Counselors must also ensure that they do not overlook serious issues, such as physical abuse, which may take more time for students to disclose. Brief counseling interventions are not suitable for problems such as suicidal ideation, abuse, and eating disorders (Littrell et al., 1995). School counselors often encounter situations in which they must mediate between family members and school personnel in a high-conflict and confrontational setting. Counselors must possess a keen awareness of their own issues to remain objective when working with troubled families. Ethically, counselors must possess a great deal of self-awareness and personal exploration to help families (Evans & Carter, 1997; Littrell et al., 1995). It is always useful and appropriate for school counselors to attend workshops that encourage further training in family systems, genogram development, and other related topics if they are working with families.

Conclusion

Assumptions underlying the solution-focused family counseling model are that the family is viewed as critical to student success; the present and future must be the focus; change will occur if strengths are emphasized and built on, rather than weaknesses or deficiencies; solutions, not problems, become the focus; and school-based family counseling is an appropriate method of helping students to solve their problems within the family framework. Advantages of the solution-focused family counseling model are increased cooperative relationships among school staff, parents, and students and time efficiency. "We school counselors have a profound effect on the lives of our students. We can have a far-reaching effect if we view those students as part of their family context and not just the individual students we see in school" (Kraus, 1998, p. 15). School counselors are ready for the challenge.

Appendix

Helpful Web Sites

American Counseling Association
URL: www.counseling.org
5999 Stevenson Avenue
Alexandria, VA 22304
Telephone: (703) 823-9800
Fax: (703) 823-0252
The American Counseling Association (ACA) is a not-for-profit professional and educational organization that is dedicated to the growth and enhancement of the counseling profession. Founded in 1952, ACA is the world's largest association exclusively representing professional counselors.

American Family Therapy Academy
URL: http://www.afta.org
2020 Pennsylvania Avenue, NW, #273
Washington, DC 20006
Telephone: (202) 333-3690
The American Family Therapy Academy is an academy of nearly 900 family therapy teachers, researchers, and practitioners who work together to continue the development of the fields of family therapy and systemic practices. It was founded as a not-for-profit tax-exempt organization by an interdisciplinary group of mental health professionals who had been active during the early years when the field of family therapy was emerging.

Brief Family Therapy Center
URL: http://www.brief-therapy.org
P. O. Box 13736
Milwaukee, WI 53213
E-mail: briefftc@aol.com
Telephone: (414) 302-0650
Fax: (414) 302-0753
A not-for-profit research and training center founded in 1978, the Brief Family Therapy Center (BFTC) has pioneered effective brief therapy methods. The model developed at the center has come to be known as solution-focused brief therapy. This model has been used successfully for more than a decade in a variety of settings including child protection agencies, community mental health clinics, private practices, sexual abuse programs, substance abuse treatment, family-based services, schools, and many other places. The model shows how to develop solutions that are generated by the client, not by the professionals.

Families USA
URL: www.familiesusa.org
1334 G Street, NW
Washington, DC 20005
Telephone: (202) 628-3030
Fax: 202 347-2417
E-mail: info@familiesusa.org
Families USA is a national nonprofit, nonpartisan organization dedicated to the achievement of high-quality and long-term health care for all Americans.

Family Re-Union
URL: www.familyreunion.org
The Family Re-Union Web site offers a collection of reports, speeches, and resources from the annual Family Reunion conferences. Family Reunion is a policy initiative informed by a series of annual conferences that are moderated by former Vice President Gore and Mrs. Gore. The conferences bring together families and those who work with them to discuss and design better ways to strengthen family life in America.

Knowledge Exchange Network (KEN)
URL: www.mentalhealth.org/cmhs/childrenscampaign/index.htm
Telephone: 1-800-789-2647
The Child, Adolescent, and Family Branch of the Federal Center

for Mental Health Services promotes and ensures that the mental health needs of children and their families are met within the context of community-based systems of care.

Positive Parenting
URL: www.positiveparenting.com/
3067 Channel Drive
Ventura, CA 93003
Telephone: (805) 642-6384
E-mail: webmaster@positiveparenting.com
This organization is dedicated to providing resources to make parenting positive, rewarding, and fun.

Stepfamily Foundation, Inc.
URL: www.stepfamily.org/
333 West End Avenue
New York, NY 10023
Telephone: (212) 877-3244
Fax: (212) 362-7030
E-mail: staff@stepfamily.org
In the best interests of the family and the child, the Stepfamily Foundation offers information on coparenting, single parents, and the stepfamily. They also offer telephone and in-person counseling as well as seminars for professionals and coaches, lectures worldwide, research, and programs for corporations.

Trinity Health
URL: http://trinity.minot.org
One West Burdick Expressway
P.O. Box 5020
Minot, ND 58702-5020
E-mail: info@minot.org
Telephone: (701) 857-5000 or toll-free (800) 862-0005
Trinity Health is northwest North Dakota's largest health care provider and a leader in medical education. As an integrated health system, Trinity Health includes physicians, clinics, a hospital, a nursing home, and other health-related services that primarily serve residents of North Dakota, Montana, and Saskatchewan. Its mission is to preserve and improve the quality of health in the region. As a community service, the organization has designed this Web site to help patients, physicians, community members, and others.

In addition, many state governments have Web sites that detail local mental health services. For example, the State of Utah's site is http://www.utah.gov/government/onlineservices.html

Excellent Print Resource

Metcalf, L. (1995). *Counseling toward solutions.* New York: Center for Applied Research in Education.

References

Amatea, E. S. (1989). *Brief strategic intervention for school behavior problems.* San Francisco: Jossey-Bass.

Beck, A. T., & Emery, G. (1985). *Anxiety disorders and phobias.* New York: Basic Books.

Budman, S. H., Hoyt, M. F., & Friedman, S. (Eds.). (1992). *The first session in brief therapy.* New York: Guilford Press.

Carter, E. A., & McGoldrick, M. (Eds.). (1980). *The family life cycle: A framework for family therapy.* New York: Gardner Press.

Carter, M. J., & Sweeney, R. C. (1994). School-based family counseling. *Educational Leadership, 23,* 17–19.

Cowie, K., & Quinn, K. (1997). Brief family therapy in the schools: A new perspective on the role of the rural school counseling professional. *The Family Journal, 5,* 57–68.

Evans, W. P., & Carter, M. J. (1997). Urban school-based family counseling: Role definition, practice applications, and training implications. *Journal of Counseling and Development, 75,* 366–374.

Fuller, M. L., & Olsen, G. (Eds.). (1998). *Home-school relations.* Needham Heights, MA: Allyn & Bacon.

Goldenberg, L., & Goldenberg, H. (2000). *Family therapy: An overview* (4th ed.). Monterey, CA: Brooks/Cole.

Hinkle, J. S. (1993). Training school counselors to do family counseling. *Elementary School Guidance and Counseling, 27,* 252–257.

Kral, R. (1990). Family therapy in the schools. *Guidance and Counseling, 5,* 19–31.

Kraus, I. (1998). A fresh look at school counseling: A family-systems approach. *Professional School Counseling, 1,* 12–17.

Lee, M. -Y. (1997). A study of solution focused brief family therapy. Outcomes and issues. *American Journal of Family Therapy, 225,* 3–17.

Lewis, W. (1996). A proposal for initiating family counseling interventions by school counselors. *The School Counselor, 44,* 93–99.

Littrell, J. M., Malia, J. A., & Vanderwood, M. (1995). Single-session brief counseling in a high school. *Journal of Counseling & Development, 73,* 451–458.

Murphy, J. J. (1994). Working with what works: A solution-focused approach to school behavior problems. *The School Counselor, 42*, 59–65.

Paisley, P. O., & Benshoff, J. M. (1996). Applying developmental principles to practice: Training issues for the professional development of school counselors. *Elementary School Guidance and Counseling, 30*, 163–169.

Selekman, M. (1991). The solution-oriented parenting group: A treatment alternative that works. *Journal of Strategic and Systematic Therapies, 10*, 36–49.

Schmidt, J. J. (1996). *Counseling in schools* (2nd ed.). Needham Heights, MA: Allyn & Bacon.

Steinberg, L. (1996). *Beyond the classroom: Why school reform has failed and what parents need to do*. New York: Simon & Schuster.

Talmon, M. (1990). *Single session therapy*. San Francisco: Jossey-Bass.

Walsh, W. M., & Giblin, N. J. (Eds.). (1988). *Family counseling in school settings*. Springfield, IL: Charles C Thomas.

Walsh, W. M., & Williams, G. R. (Eds.). (1997). *Schools and family therapy*. Springfield, IL: Charles C Thomas.

■ ■ ■

4

Compendium of Practices for Including Children in Family Sessions

Alan Carr, PhD

This chapter contains a compendium of proven research-based and clinic-based techniques for use in family counseling in school settings. Each technique is discussed and suggestions are given for implementation. These techniques are appropriate with any age, from preschool children to adolescents. Some of the techniques are also helpful for adults because they make the abstract concrete. A good counselor adjusts the level of discussion and elevation of vocabulary to fit the maturity of each child. Topics include

- making the therapeutic context attractive,
- explaining the therapeutic process and systemic ideas in concrete terms,
- tracking patterns of interaction using dolls and drawings,
- using genograms and lifelines to assess perception of family structure and development,
- using face drawings to assess perception of emotional atmosphere,
- inviting the child to draw a picture of the future,
- tracking perceived changes using visual analogue scales,

- teaching turn taking,
- using personification and externalization of problems and strengths to solve or reframe problems,
- using stories and metaphors,
- coaching children in new skills, and
- providing children with advocacy.

Making the Context Attractive

Children and adolescents can be initially threatened by family counseling. Their anxiety may be reduced by arranging a child-oriented area in the waiting room and by offering refreshments, such as orange juice and cookies. After each session young children may be given a sticker with a smiling face or another positive image. After a complete course of family counseling, children may be given a certificate to show that they have completed the counseling program.

Explaining the Process and Ideas in Concrete Terms

Children's anxiety about counseling may be reduced by explaining in concrete terms the role they will be expected to play in counseling and what counseling will involve in concrete terms. This also helps them to contribute to the process more productively. In the following example the therapist explains the consultation process to a 6-year-old with abdominal pain for which no physical basis could be found.

Therapist: You and I and your mom and dad are going to talk together in this room for about an hour or so. That's the same length of time as *Sesame Street*. Do you watch *Sesame Street?*

Child: Yes. Sometimes at Granny's.

Therapist: Your mom and dad told me that they are worried about the pain you are getting in your tummy. You know the one.

Child: (Nods.) Mmm.

Therapist: Well, I may be able to help you with that. OK?

Child: (Nods. Looks tearful.) Mmm.

Therapist: But the thing is this, I want you to know that I can help you to feel better. But here I don't give injections or use pills to make tummy aches better. Were you worried about that?

Child: Yes. I don't like needles.

Therapist: Sometimes I ask people to do special exercises and things to help them get rid of aches and pains.

Child: What sort of exercises?

Therapist: The boy I saw this morning had to do some deep breathing exercises with his mom. I'll see him again next week to check how he got on with the exercises. Do you do breathing exercises in PE?

Child: Sometimes.

Therapist: OK. So you know what I mean. But first I want you to draw a picture of yourself and show me where the pain is on the picture and what color it feels like.

Systemic concepts that underpin family counseling and the language used to express systemic ideas are complex. Nevertheless, if children are to participate fully in family counseling, it may be important for them to understand some of these complex ideas, such as the interdependence of family members, the cumulative effects of stress, and the effects of criticism and emotional overinvolvement. These are best addressed through the use of concrete models.

The Mobile

A fish mobile is a useful way to explain interdependence. Siblings of referred children often ask why they have to attend counseling if they are not sick, sad, or bad. Ask them to move one fish on the fish family mobile hanging in the office. Ask if this affected the other fish. This leads to an exploration of how the sibling's problems affect everyone in the family and how the family can help the sibling solve the problems.

The Balloon

When youngsters are under pressure, they may be given a balloon to blow into each time a stress factor that affects them is mentioned. The therapist then engages the rest of the family in an exploration of stressors that the youngster faces. Eventually the balloon bursts, dramatizing the cumulative effects of the various stressors on the child. When parents have difficulty empathizing with the stressors a child faces, this is a particularly valuable intervention.

The Scale

When parents criticize one child exclusively and ignore the shortcomings of the other children, a plastic balancing scale designed for teaching math concepts is a useful way of dramatizing the effects of this on the children. Each child can have a turn using the scale while the therapist asks the parents about that child's daily behavior. The child holding the scale must put one counter on the right side each time the parents say a positive remark and one counter on the left side for each critical comment. The unbalanced amount of criticism that the scapegoated child has to bear becomes evident, and the need for balance in praise and criticism can then be explored.

The Rope

When a parent continually talks for a child, the child may be asked to hold one end of a rope while the parent holds the other end. Each time the child notices the parent talking for him or her, the child pulls the rope. This is a useful method for reducing enmeshment and emotional overinvolvement.

Tracking Patterns of Interaction

Tracking sequences of interaction with children is a useful way of including them in counseling. Often children notice things in behavioral sequences that adults are unaware of or will not admit to seeing. Important sequences are those in which the presenting problem is embedded and those exceptional patterns of interaction that are slightly different but in which the problem does not occur. Comparing these sequences may then throw light on ways in which the problem may be resolved. With young children these sequences may be dramatized using dolls or puppets, or they may be drawn on a white board or flip chart. This helps children to keep whole sequences of interaction in memory when two or more sequences are being compared. This technique also allows children to express things that they may not be able to express in words.

Using Genograms and Lifelines

The genogram and family lifeline, longstanding family evaluation methods, offer many opportunities for children to be involved in counseling, particularly if these assessment methods are described as games. Drawing a genogram is a game, the object of which is to draw a map of everyone in the family. The rules state that squares are for boys, circles for girls. Every circle or square must have a name and an age in it. The therapist then asks questions as if conducting a game show quiz. The therapist can ask individual children, or the family can be divided into teams, with adults and children answering questions for their team. During the process of drawing a genogram, gaps in family members' knowledge and differences of opinion about family life may become apparent and require further inquiry. When the basic genogram is finished, more detailed information about key family members may be included and patterns identified.

A developmental family history can be represented pictorially on the white board as a family lifeline. A game show quiz format may be used to involve the children in contributing to its construction. Gaps in knowledge and discrepancies between accounts may be explored when the lifeline is complete. An example of a genogram is given in Figure 4.1, and an example of a lifeline is presented in Figure 4.2.

Using Face Drawings

The counselor draws faces—like those presented in Figure 4.3—that represent four emotions on a white board and asks the children in the family what emotions the faces represent. Then the

FIGURE 4.1
A Genogram

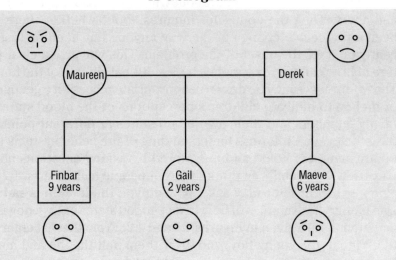

FIGURE 4.2
A Lifeline

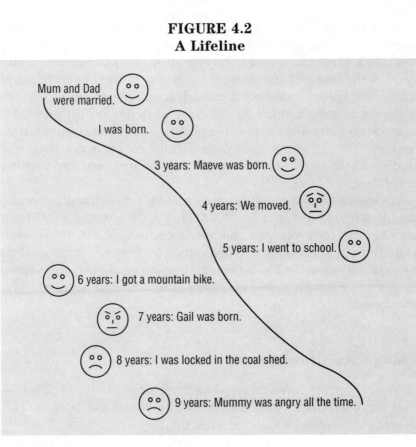

counselor asks the children, one at a time, to give their opinion
about who is most sad, happy, scared, and angry now. The counselor follows this with questions about who is least sad, happy, scared,
and angry. Then the counselor inquires about whether there has
been a noticeable change in the way anyone has been feeling recently or since the onset of the problem. This will give a clear picture of how children experience the emotional climate of the family.
These four faces may be drawn in appropriate places on a genogram
or lifeline to indicate children's perceptions of the mood states of
family members and their own mood states at different points in
their life cycle. Children's understanding of the belief systems that
family members hold can be explored by asking questions about
why each of the children think different people feel differently. For
example a counselor may ask, "Why do you think Mom is sad but
Dad is angry?" Examples of how to map mood states onto genograms
and lifelines are given in Figures 4.1 and 4.2. From these it emerged
that Finbar, the young boy who drew them, felt that he and his father were sad because they were excluded from a relationship with

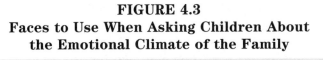

FIGURE 4.3
Faces to Use When Asking Children About
the Emotional Climate of the Family

Maureen since the birth of Gail. The difficulties associated with this seemed to lead Maeve, his 6-year-old sister, to be worried or scared. He loved school from the day he started, and all of the difficulties seemed to be home based.

Inviting Children to Draw the Future

A particularly engaging way to help children describe their goals in concrete terms is to ask them to draw a picture of the family as it would be in 6 months' time if everything worked out right for them. Then, interview them about what each person in the family is thinking, feeling, and doing. A variation on this technique is to ask the children to draw a picture of their family as it is now and as it would be in 6 months' time if everything turned out right. Then ask them to highlight the differences between the two pictures. In particular, how are the beliefs, feelings, and actions of family members different?

Finbar, the boy whose genogram and lifeline are given in Figures 4.1 and 4.2, portrayed his future with him sitting beside his mom on the couch, with Derek holding Gail, and with Maeve sitting on the floor. All family members were watching television and laughing. The shed had been converted into a playroom, and there was a computer that Finbar could use whenever he liked.

Tracking Perceived Changes

Tracking a client's perception of change is a crucial aspect of counseling. Discussion of perceived change provides feedback necessary for developing more adaptive ways of coping. Visual techniques are particularly useful in helping young children describe and discuss their perception of changes, in both the symptom and the family system.

Visual analogue scales are useful for helping children express perceived changes in the intensity of a problem or an emotion. They are particularly useful for detecting changes in pain, fear, anger, sadness, and happiness. They can also be used to help children express changes in interpersonal factors, such as how close children feel to their mother or how warm they feel about a family member. To use visual analogue scales meaningfully, anchor points must be agreed upon and held constant from session to session. Here is an example to illustrate the process:

Therapist: You see this line? It goes from 1 to 10. Now, I want to know how sad or happy you've been feeling since last week. OK?

Child: Just a bit sad.

Therapist: OK. You said that last week, so I'm going to ask you to use this line to help me see if you still feel the same or different. Worse or better. Now, 1 stands for the sadness you felt when you had to go into hospital. Do you remember that feeling?

Child: Yes. I was really sad then.

Therapist: 10 is how you felt in Spain last year. Really happy. OK? One is sad in the hospital, and 10 is happy in Spain. Got that?

Child: Yes.

Therapist: Put a mark on the line for how sad you are now.

Child: Mmmm . . . here.

Therapist: Now put in a mark for how you felt last week. Better or worse than now?

Bar charts are useful for tracking changes in symptoms or events that can be expressed as frequencies, such as the number of nightmares, the number of times a youngster vomited, the number of tantrums, or the number of fires set. These are of most value if the parents keep an ongoing record of the events as they occur. Then in each session the child can draw a bar chart for each week on the board and see the change in frequency.

Teaching Turn Taking

Silent children and disruptive children have difficulty participating in counseling. In both cases there is a need to introduce a concrete method for showing that it is the child's turn to speak. In Golding's *Lord of the Flies*, children in council meetings were only allowed to speak if they held the conch, a large sea shell that symbolized authority. This practice is also useful in family counseling. The rules of turn taking need to be clearly spelled out. Everybody gets a turn. When it's a person's turn, he or she holds the conch and speaks. No one can interrupt. The therapist can interrupt if the person speaks for more than 4 minutes. When a person has finished talking, he or she hands the conch back to the therapist who then passes it to the person whose turn it is next.

Using Personification and Externalization to Solve Problems

Many psychological difficulties involve internal conflict: The person feels torn between two sets of feelings, beliefs, or courses of action. An important part of counseling is to articulate the conflicting inner states and then explore alternatives for handling the dilemma. Children (and indeed many adults) find the process of externalizing these competing inner states and naming them as people useful in managing this process. The following example illustrates this technique:

> Theresa, a 9-year-old, was sent to the counselor's office because she consistently failed to complete her homework, despite staying up studying until after 10 p.m. most evenings. She looked pale and tired during the initial session. She said she wanted to finish her homework, but the harder she tried to finish it, the less she got done. She was a very bright girl with an excellent academic record. Her difficulty confused her, her parents, and her teachers. The counselor asked her to write a brief essay about her family in the session and to tell the counselor what she was thinking when she became stuck. With careful prompting, she eventually identified how her need to improve each sentence she composed in her mind was preventing her from writing fluently. She externalized this urge by translating it into one half of a dialogue with the part of herself that wanted to write the essay. Here is part of the dialogue:

> There are four people in my family.
> No, that's not quite right.
> In my family there are my parents, my brother Paul, and myself.
> No, that's the wrong way to start. What about the house?
> My family lives in a bungalow in Malahide.

> The counselor then invited Theresa to personify this urge to reedit everything she composed. She named the urge Miss Right. The

goal of counseling became developing a relationship with Miss Right so that Theresa could ask her to go away and let her do her homework in peace and then come in afterwards and check that it was correct, rather than hovering over every sentence.

The externalization and personification of urges to engage in problem behavior is useful for obsessive-compulsive disorders, such as Theresa's, and for phobias, tics, enuresis, and encopresis. The key to working with urges to engage in negative behavior is not to destroy this aspect of the self but to make friends with it and integrate it into the child's sense of self.

Strengths and competencies can also be externalized and personified. Aggressive children who need to learn temper control or shy children who need to learn assertiveness may begin by externalizing and personifying a character that has these new skills. The child can then be invited to let this character have a place in his or her life. The following example shows this technique:

> Trevor, age 10, was extremely shy and had difficulty making friends. However, he was a good cyclist. During counseling, he developed a character called The Spin. The Spin was a brilliant cyclist and trickster who loved cycling with other people. However, he only talked to people about bikes. No matter what you said to The Spin, he always answered in terms of cycling. So, if a person said "Hello," The Spin said "Hi, great day for wheelies." If a person said, "Goodbye," The Spin said "Bye, and hope you never get a puncture." For homework the counselor asked Trevor to cycle to the playground each day, gradually increasing periods of time, and pretend to be The Spin. He found that when he did this, he was able to overcome his shyness. Eventually, he made two close friends. They talked a lot about bikes at first, but later Trevor found that he talked about other things, too. He no longer needed to pretend to be The Spin with his friends. However, he brought The Spin back into his life whenever he felt threatened or shy.

Counselors can also externalize and personify aspects of themselves to help engage children in counseling. Andrew Wood's (1988) cotherapist, King Tiger, is a delightful example of this approach. Andrew tells children that he will talk to King Tiger about their problems or strengths. King Tiger then writes the child a letter that Andrew delivers. The letters are all written from a child's viewpoint and may be used to help the child reframe his or her situation, identify personal strengths, acknowledge accomplishments, and so forth. The child is encouraged to write back to King Tiger and build a pen-pal relationship.

Using Stories and Metaphors

The use of parables, myths, and fairy tales to help people find solutions to problems of living is a custom that has its roots in the oral storytelling tradition. The key to good practice in this area is to take the salient elements of the client's situation and build them into a story that arrives at a conclusion that offers the client an avenue toward productive change, rather than a painful cul-de-sac. The story is a metaphor for the client's dilemma, a metaphor that offers a solution. This age-old technique is particularly useful for involving children in counseling. The following is an example of this technique:

Sabina, a 7-year-old girl, was sent to the counselor's office because of recurrent nightmares in which she dreamed her house was being burglarized and her parents assaulted. The nightmares followed an actual burglary of the family's shop, over which they lived. The girl dealt with the nightmares by climbing onto the end of her parents' bed—so as not to wake them—and trying to think of something else. During the day she refused to talk about the nightmares or the burglary. To some degree, her parents went along with this process of denial. Sabina was in Brownies and was learning about first aid when she was referred. Toward the end of the first session, the counselor told the following story:

Two Brownie scouts were on an adventure in the woods. They decided to have a race. They were both the same height and looked alike, except one had blond hair like yours, and one had dark hair. While they were racing—and they were neck and neck all the way—they both tripped over the same branch, and each girl cut her knee. The cuts hurt a lot, and both girls felt like crying. The dark-haired girl tried to stop herself from crying, and her leg hurt more. The blond girl allowed herself to cry and felt relieved. The crying made her knee hurt less. Both girls went to the stream and bathed their cuts. Both girls had small first-aid kits in their pockets. The dark-haired girl put a bandage from her kit on her cut straight away. The blond girl could have done this also, but she did not. She let her cut air. Both girls went home for tea. After tea they went to bed. The dark-haired girl couldn't sleep because the cut hurt so much. She turned on the light. She took off the bandage and noticed that the cut had become infected. It was all yellow with puss. The dark-haired girl washed the cut quickly and put another bandage over the puss. The blond girl woke in the middle of the night because her knee was hurting her. She woke her mom and her mom helped her bathe the cut in hot water to draw the puss out. This was painful, but she knew it would make her better. Three days later her cut was better, but her friend was still wearing a bandage. Her knee still had puss in it. She still woke up in the middle of the night with the pain.

In the conversation that followed, Sabina and her parents began to talk openly about the robbery and the nightmares, and the parents spontaneously invited Sabina to wake them when she had nightmares. The counselor asked Sabina to draw pictures of the nightmares and explain them to her parents and the counselor. After three sessions, over a period of a month, the nightmares had almost disappeared.

This story took account of Sabina's interest in first aid and racing. A physical trauma (cutting her knee) was used as a metaphor for the psychological trauma she had suffered (being burglarized). The story included one course of action taken by the dark-haired girl, which resembled the pattern of coping she had adopted. It also contained an alternative. The blond girl, whose hair was the color of Sabrina's, took this other more adaptive route. The hair color was chosen to make it easy for Sabina to identify with her. The story reframed Sabina's dilemma from "How can I distract myself from memories of the robbery and get rid of these nightmares so I can feel good?" to "How can I squeeze all of this psychological puss out of my mind so the wound will heal?" This reframing offered a new avenue for coping.

Coaching Children in New Skills

Children delight in mastering new skills. This may be capitalized on in family counseling by using sessions as a forum for teaching new skills that are to be practiced as homework. Commonly these new skills involve interacting with parents in particular ways. With young children this coaching process can be applied to teaching children to play a variety of games or engage in a variety of activities with their parents, while avoiding unnecessary conflict. The skills include checking if the parent is available to play, planning an alternative time if the parent is unavailable, selecting a game, asking the parent to select a game, following rules, accepting interruptions without tantrums, accepting that the special time period is limited, showing appreciation, and arranging to play again. With young children, behavioral parenting skills—such as using time out or token systems—can be taught with a high degree of child involvement if they are reframed as helping the child to learn self-control or self-directed behavior. The following example illustrates this technique:

Sean, a 6-year-old, was referred to counseling because of tantrums and defiance. A time out and token system was developed with him and his parents. His temper was personified and externalized as Mister Fire. We spent some time talking about how hard it was for Sean to control Mister Fire and how useful it would be to be able to do so. It would help him to avoid conflicts with his parents. It would prevent him from feeling shame, and in sports he could ask Mister Fire to help him to run fast and kick the soccer ball harder. At the close of this conversation, Sean said he wished he could learn to control Mister Fire. The counselor explained that any time Mister Fire started coming out and making Sean be rude or naughty, he should run up to his room, let Mister Fire have a good shout and then tell him to calm down. Sean agreed to do this. I said that he would need his mother's help sometimes. She could remind him to bring Mister Fire upstairs or help him get Mister Fire back into the room if he escaped before he had calmed down. She agreed to this.

To tackle the problem of defiance, the counselor first worked on Sean's refusal to tidy his toys up each evening. He loved to go to the adventure playground on weekends with his father, but this rarely happened. We discussed the playground at length and what incentives Dad might need to bring him there. After some prompting, Sean suggested that dad would love a Saturday newspaper that cost $1.00. The question was what chores Sean could do to earn this. A number were explored, and Sean and his parents settled on tidying the playroom each night at 6:00 p.m. Mom would pay him a quarter if he completed the job successfully.

The parents kept routine behavioral records. The frequency of tantrums decreased rapidly after an initial increase, and Sean regularly tidied the toys up for 6 weeks. He also began to take responsibility in other areas.

In this example, the parents implemented routine behavioral time out and token programs. However, Sean participated in their development and implementation. He also construed them as an opportunity to learn how to control his temper and how to arrange to go the adventure playground with his father.

Providing Children With Advocacy

In complex multiproblem cases, especially if there is multiagency involvement, there is a danger that the child's voice will become lost in the complexities of the problem-determined system. This is often true of cases involving child abuse, foster care, parental criminality or psychiatric difficulties, bereavement, hospitalization, or special education. Providing the child with a key worker or advocate in such situations is an important way of ensuring that the child may participate in family counseling or broader systemic consultation meetings in a meaningful way. The advocate may involve the child in a series of individual sessions to help clarify the child's point of view. The advocate may then help the child present this view in family or network consultations. The following example shows how to incorporate advocacy:

> Cindy was originally referred for neuropsychological assessment and counseling by the pediatrics department in a district hospital in the United Kingdom following a road traffic accident in which she sustained a closed head injury and in which her father was killed. Subsequently, her mother, Christine, a poorly controlled diabetic, had great difficulty caring for Cindy (age 9) and her younger brother, Kevin (age 6). After a year, and a series of crises in which Christine was unable to cope with the children, respite care was arranged with social services. Cindy and Kevin spent between 2 and 4 days a week with foster parents in a nearby village. This respite care evolved into full-time care when Christine was hospitalized for surgery following the diagnosis of breast cancer. When Christine was discharged from the hospital, an agreement was reached that the children should stay in full-time care but that they would have regular visits with Christine, who felt unable to cope with them on a full-time basis. In addition to the stress of bereavement, single parenthood, poorly controlled diabetes, and cancer, Christine was also engaged in litigation for compensation in relation to the accident in which her husband was killed and her daughter injured. Throughout 5 years, more than 30 professionals were involved in this case. These included pediatricians, family doctors, psychiatrists, nurses, occupational therapists, physical therapists, social workers, remedial teachers, insurance agents, lawyers, foster parents, home aid workers, and managers from the departments of social services and education. Many of the systemic consultation meetings that were convened involved up to a dozen of these professionals, along with Cindy, Kevin, and Christine. A key element in involving both Cindy and Kevin in these consultations and allowing their opinions and views to be heard was providing them with advocacy throughout the process.

Conclusion

The approach to involving children in family counseling described here is based on three principles. First, at an ethical level, children have a right to participate in the process of solving the problems of living that they and their families face. Second, at a pragmatic level, counseling has a better chance of success if those involved in the problem, including children, participate in the solution. Third, at a theoretical level, methods of engaging children in counseling must be based on an integration of therapeutic practices and an appreciation of the psychology of child development. A fuller account of the use of these techniques in the practice of family therapy and child and adolescent clinical psychology is contained elsewhere (Carr, 1999, 2000).

References

Carr, A. (1999). *Handbook of clinical child psychology: A contextual approach.* London: Routledge.

Carr, A. (2000). *Family therapy: Concepts, process, and practice.* Chichester, UK: Wiley.

Wood, A. (1988). King Tiger and the roaring tummies: A novel way of helping young children and their families change. *Journal of Family Therapy, 10,* 49–63.

■ ■ ■

5

Including Parents and Teachers

Deanna Hawes, PhD

Fuller (1998) has described the relationship between parents and teachers as having an interesting history that parallels the economic history of our country. The U.S. economy has changed dramatically since the 1970s and so has the relationship between educators and parents. More families are realizing it takes two salaries to provide a home. Single-parent families are greater in number than are traditional, two-parent–one-income households. Consequently, to maintain a middle-class standard of living, most mothers of school children are a part of the workforce. In contrast to previous generations, the majority of women with children under 5 years of age work away from the home (Barr & Parrett, 1995). Therefore, many parents are participating less often in school functions. With less parental involvement in the schools, it is important that greater knowledge and understanding of the family compensate for a meaningful relationship between the school and the home (Fuller, 1998). Parent involvement currently is designed to encourage parents to interact more with the school. Parental involvement is vital to the success of school counseling programs at all levels. School counselors need to make every effort to establish lines of communication with the parents, invite parents to help plan their children's education goals, and provide services for the family (Schmidt, 1999). It is important that parents, teachers, and school counselors become team members in the education of their children.

The National Education Goals Panel (1994) listed one of eight goals, which was to have been achieved by the year 2000, as follows: "Every school will promote partnerships that will increase parental involvement and participation in promoting the social, emotional, and academic growth of children." Studies conducted by Henderson and Berla (1994) indicated that when parents are involved in children's education at school, the results include one or more of the following:

- higher grades and test scores,
- better attendance and regularly completed homework,
- fewer placements in special education or remedial classes,
- more positive attitudes and behaviors in school,
- higher graduation rates, and
- greater enrollment in postsecondary education.

School districts need to establish and implement parent-involvement policies, with input from parents. Counselors can help with the development of these policies.

It is important that teachers understand the families from which their students come. Students bring their family experiences with them to school. Therefore, it is important that teachers have a good understanding of the family, so they can better understand the child. It is most helpful to the child's education if the parents and teachers work together as a team. Teachers and parents have often been referred to as "natural allies" (McDonald, 1998). They share a common goal of wanting children to develop to their full potential. But despite their common goal, teachers and parents don't always work comfortably together. The role of the school counselor is to help parents and teachers understand each other and connect to each other. It is important for the counselor to help parents and teachers revitalize their communication and maintain a bond that will serve to guide children in their learning. School counselors can help provide opportunities for developing better relationships between parents and teachers.

Specific Strategies for Developing Cooperative Relationships Between Parents and Teachers

Parent–Teacher Communication

School counselors can help parents and teachers form strong partnerships to maximize the benefit of parent involvement. This task is not always easy to achieve. It requires mutual commitment, action, trust, and understanding from parents and teachers (Hanhan, 1998). One of the first steps teachers can take toward successful parent involvement is to learn the basic skills of communication. Counselors are trained in active listening skills, "I" messages, empathic responding, and other communication skills. These skills need to be taught to teachers.

Currently most parent–teacher communication tends to be a one-way written method, of teacher to parent, with an expectation that parents will receive teacher wisdom. Examples of this one-way communication are newsletters, parent handbooks, orientation meetings, and report cards. These typically involve the teacher telling parents about activities, school policies and procedures, and student progress. Similarly, parent–teacher conferences are often viewed as opportunities to tell parents how their children are doing in school. To have better parent involvement, parents must be encouraged to speak and to be heard (Hanhan, 1998). Communication must flow in two ways, and for this to happen both parents and teachers must consider each other in a respectful manner. This can be achieved through effective communication skills, which counselors can teach. The following list includes the principles of effective communication (Hanhan, 1990):

- Choose or create an environment that puts parents and teachers on an equal footing (this may or may not be the teacher's classroom).
- Listen to understand—use active listening skills.
- Use descriptive, rather than judgmental language when relating a child's school life.
- Refrain from talking about other parents or their children—either in positive or negative terms. Respect the confidentiality of all families.
- Take the initiative to establish a co-equal relationship—ask parents to help provide solutions.
- Establish communications early in the school year, before problems occur.
- Find time to spend with parents.

It is possible for teachers to affect the nature of their relationships with the parents of their students. Most parents and many teachers consider schools to be teacher territory, not parent territory. Many parents view teachers as authority figures, the expert in teaching and learning, and they are often uncertain about their own expertise in parenting (MacDonald, 1998). Counselors can remind teachers that it is the teacher's responsibility to first contact the parent, and they can set the stage for an equal partnership. Unfortunately, this is not always easy because there are many barriers that need to be avoided or overcome. If teachers merely use the previously mentioned communication techniques with parents at the initial contact (e.g., "Mrs. Brown, I would like to spend as much time as we need discussing Jessica's performance"), this often can establish a positive, collaborative atmosphere.

Language often poses a number of stumbling blocks for teachers and parents wishing to establish two-way communication. Mutual understanding requires both clear articulation on the part of the speaker and accurate interpretation on the part of the listener. Hanhan (1998) provided the following example: A teacher told the parent in a parent-teacher conference that her child was "what we call immature." When the parent inquired further about his immaturity, the teacher said that, "he was reluctant to try new things." The parent asked what he was reluctant to do. The teacher said he was unwilling to climb some bleachers. At this point, the teacher's comments made sense to the mother because she knew her son was frightened by heights; only now could she be of some help to the teacher in offering both an explanation and the beginnings of a solution. When education language or jargon is used, many parents can be left feeling inept, ashamed, or even stupid to ask for an explanation. Hanhan (1998) suggested that it is better for teachers to forego jargon of all kinds in favor of using everyday language that is specific, concrete, and free of value judgments.

Nonverbal Messages

The use of nonverbal messages can also complicate the communication process. Body positions (e.g., arms and legs folded tightly), gestures (e.g., a shrug of the shoulders), facial expressions (e.g., a quivering lip or flaring nostrils), tone of voice or rate of speech (e.g., a firm and monotone voice), or an involuntary behavior (e.g., a quick inhale of breath) can all carry signals to the listener. If our nonverbal behaviors do not correspond with the message we wish to convey, or if we are unfamiliar with the meanings on nonverbal behaviors in other cultures, these behaviors can become obstacles to clear communication. Body language can provide information about a person's emotional state (Brammer, 1988). A person who has their arms folded and quickly turns away is most likely upset;

this can be useful information. However, we do not want to overinterpret every movement.

Teachers sometimes deal with parents who are exhibiting contradictory nonverbal messages. For example, while talking with a parent who has a calm voice, the parent may be smiling while tears run down his or her face. In situations such as this the teacher can say something to reflect the feeling—for example, "I noticed that while we were talking about Beth's math scores you were upset." Feelings are frequently expressed in behavior, rather than words.

Active Listening

A key to establishing a relationship in which two or more people communicate effectively is active listening. Counselors can teach parents and teachers that being a good listener requires the use of verbal and nonverbal skills. It involves eye contact and a posture that indicates the person is listening. Listening requires close attention to what the individual is saying and concentration on the meaning of both words and action. It may be helpful to ask the question, "What is really important?" to the individual as he or she is talking. Through close attention the teacher may then communicate recognition of the feelings behind the words. This skill, reflection of feeling, is one that communicates the understanding of what has been heard (Brammer, 1988). Reflection of feeling involves an attempt to understand what the individual feels and means, and then state this meaning so the person feels understood and accepted. Reflecting feeling focuses on both words and behavior. It should be noted that the nonverbal part of the communication is provided through the behavior. Reflecting feeling is nonjudgmental, helps identify the real problem, and encourages the individual to feel heard and to continue talking. Active listening on the part of the teacher can communicate a wish to engage in a two-way communication. When the teacher begins to listen and respond with empathy and understanding, mutual trust and respect begin to develop.

Written Communication

Written communication can be formal or informal. If it is written, it needs to have correct spelling. In communities that use a second language, consider having two publications: one in standard English and the same communication translated into the other language or languages of the community. One of the most common methods of written communication with parents is a newsletter. Newsletters are published regularly to inform parents of the events in the classroom. One method teachers can use to encourage parents to read the newsletter is to be sure to write something about each child in the class, highlighting children's names (Hanhan, 1998). This is true for both the elementary and secondary levels. Ideally, newsletters should not be more than two pages long. Parents are very busy and may feel overwhelmed by a multipage document. The newsletter provides the teacher with an opportunity to share with parents the exciting things that are occurring in the classroom. It is important to use students' work, articles written by students, and illustrations drawn by students (Hanhan, 1998). It is important to include as many students in the newsletter as possible, eventually including all students in future editions. At the high school level, for instance, the mathematics teacher can have a subject-focused newsletter with project deadlines, outstanding students, interesting concepts, and so forth. Counselors and teachers need to consider effective ways of involving parents in writing and printing the newsletter. Perhaps a parent can contribute career information or a useful application of geometry in his or her workplace. This activity provides opportunities for parental involvement and may identify more items parents would like to see in the newsletter.

Another form for two-way written communication is a school-home journal. This is especially helpful when parents cannot visit the school on a regular basis. A school-home journal is a notebook in which teachers make comments about the child's school day. The notebook is sent home with the child, and the parent or parents respond to the teacher's comments on the child's day. Its success depends on the relationship between the parent and teacher. A parent may not be able to write in the journal every day but may find the time to do so at least twice during the week for elementary students, less frequently for secondary students. The child can be encouraged to write or draw his or her own entry into the journal. Children can help remind parents and teachers about their commitment to the journal (Hanhan, 1998).

Many parents are used to receiving the traditional report card as a way of comparing their child with other students. Teachers who write additional narrative reports for parents have increased parental appreciation and support. However, the narrative report can be time-consuming for the teachers. A good narrative report is a detailed description of the child and the child's contributions to the classroom (Hanhan, 1998). The narrative report can provide the parent a better understanding of the child's work. At the secondary level, the teacher can dictate this narrative to the student who records this in a student day planner, and then the teacher can sign it before it goes home. This is more time efficient for secondary teachers and also serves to reinforce to the older student the message that the teacher is emphasizing. A checklist of behaviors can also be effective: The secondary teacher develops expectations and evaluates the students on these expectations weekly. These weekly comments should be made for students who are excelling as well as those having difficulties.

Home Visits

Home visits at the beginning of the school year can establish good communication between parents and teachers. Parents generally appreciate the teacher's effort to visit their home. The home visit provides the parents with the opportunity to be in a place where they are in charge and where the teacher is a guest in a strange place (Hanhan, 1998). Counselors can prepare teachers for these feelings. The feelings of unease a parent may have in a school setting can be similar to a teacher's unease at being in an unfamiliar environment. Making a home visit often signals to the parent that the teacher is interested in the family and in forming a partnership in the education of the child. Children are often pleased with the presence of their teacher in their home, and they are ready to start the school year enthusiastically (Hanhan, 1998). Teachers do have a need for some caution related to home visits because of safety reasons. It is important to allow parents to refuse a home visit. Sometimes it is helpful to do home visits in pairs. The school counselor and teacher would be an ideal pair for the first visit to the home.

Communication With Groups

The school counselor is able to facilitate parent-teacher discussion groups that can help parents and teachers connect. Good times for scheduling parent/teacher groups are weekends and early evenings. If the goal is to bring parents and teachers together to address their relationship, announcements can be sent home from the school, or the program may be advertised through the media. Once the program has been announced and parents and teachers come together as a group, it is helpful to engage in some preliminary activities before introducing the primary goal of involving parents and teachers with each other. An outline of a sequence of activities in the program directed by counselors is as follows. Note that if high conflict already exists, the counselor needs to get commitment to the process of conflict resolution by screening participants individually prior to starting any group.

Establishing a foundation. Start the meeting with a warm-up or get-to-know-you activity so that all participants can feel at ease and welcome. Suggest that one of the teachers be responsible for this segment of the program.

Enhancing interpersonal communication skills. Introduce the topic of the typical distance that develops between parents and teachers. Remind the participants that listening is the primary skill necessary for good communication and the language of acceptance. Being a good listener requires eye contact and a posture that indicates the person is listening. Listening requires close attention to what each individual is saying and concentration on the meaning of both verbal and nonverbal messages. It may be helpful to ask the question, "What is really important to the parent or teacher as he or she is talking?" Through close attention to each other, parents and teachers may then communicate an understanding of one another. An excellent activity to use to help parents and teachers with their listening is "The Eyes Have It," which was presented in the program called *Innerchange: A Journey Into Self-Learning Through Interaction* (Ball, 1977). Briefly stated, this activity begins with a discussion of the points identified at the beginning of this section. The activity includes an integrative discussion and dramatizes the importance of effective listening and recognizing areas where listening breaks down.

Communication skills activity. The counselor can begin the activity by stressing that everyone has strengths and areas to improve. Communication between parents and teachers is not always easy. The counselor can initiate an activity by first reviewing Gordon's (1970) communication roadblocks:

1. ordering, commanding, directing;
2. warning, threatening;
3. moralizing, preaching, giving "shoulds" and "oughts";
4. advising, offering solutions or suggestions;
5. teaching, lecturing, giving logical arguments;
6. judging, criticizing, disagreeing, blaming;
7. name-calling, stereotyping, labeling;

8. interpreting, analyzing, diagnosing;
9. praising, agreeing, giving positive evaluations;
10. reassuring, sympathizing, consoling, supporting;
11. questioning, probing, interrogating, cross-examining; and
12. withdrawing, distracting, being sarcastic, humoring, diverting. (pp. 41–44)

Using the parents' and teachers' thoughts about their last unsatisfactory discussion, the counselor places the parents and teachers in small groups and asks them to discuss their ideas about the purpose of roadblocks in communicating with each other. Once the parents and teachers have examined the roadblocks through their own examples, the counselor brings them back to the large group and asks for the most common examples of roadblocks parents and teachers introduce into the communication.

Problem solving. It is natural for parents and teachers to have differences of opinions, and they will experience conflict. Both parents and teachers have views of what they expect or think is right about certain issues in the child's education and in the family. How we handle the relationship through these areas of conflict is a matter of how we communicate. To meet a mutually satisfying resolution to the conflict, we must go beyond listening to working through the issue. To work through the issue involves problem solving.

The following is a model for solving problems:

1. Understand the problem.
2. Consider the alternatives.
3. Select the best mutual alternative.
4. Discuss the probable results of the chosen solution.
5. Follow-up.

Consulting Model for Parent–Teacher Communication

Consultation is an intervention strategy that the school counselor could use to help parents and teachers communicate. Because parents and teachers provide most of the children's environmental experiences, effective interaction between parents and teachers will maximize opportunities for the children's growth and development. School counselors have the competence to teach various communication skills. This competence allows them to be able to show respect, confidence, and faith in others. Counselors have the ability to teach others to listen to and attend to feelings and behaviors and to handle critical incidents that add to their ability to be consultants to teachers.

The goal of consultation is the creation of positive change. Consultation follows a process. Dustin and Ehly (1984) designed a consultation model that is representative of the consultation process. The model consists of the following five stages:

- *Stage one: Phasing in.* This is primarily relationship building. The counselor needs to develop and be able to exhibit specific relationship skills, such as listening, understanding, and empathy.
- *Stage two: Problem identification.* The priority of the counselor is to help clarify the main problem between parent and teacher. The appropriate skill during this stage is focus. Additional skills include paraphrasing, restatement, goal setting (establishing priorities), and obtaining commitment.
- *Stage three: Implementation of consultation.* The counselor helps the parent or parents and the teacher explore strategies to solve the identified problem. An important skill is the ability to give feedback. Additional skills include dealing with resistance, patience, and flexibility. The counselor provides a recommendation for action.
- *Stage four: Evaluation.* The counselor evaluates how things are going. The evaluation stage ends when the parent or parents and the teacher are satisfied with the outcomes of the process. This stage involves monitoring implementation and evaluation strategies.
- *Stage five: Termination.* The school counselor signifies an ending to the consultation by bringing closure to a consultation agreement. The counselor reviews the positive and the negative outcomes derived from the strategy and provides feedback.

Consultation is an appropriate and worthwhile activity for school counselors. School counselors as consultants have an important role in creating positive change and facilitating growth and development.

Encouragement

The process of encouragement is based on communication skills and is designed to help improve sense of self (Dreikurs & Soltz, 1964). All people want to succeed at the activities they undertake.

This is a natural desire on the part of human beings. Unfortunately many individuals are discouraged. It has been the typical approach in our society to help people to learn by pointing out their mistakes. The catchphrase has been "we learn from our mistakes." What is often overlooked with the motivational strategy is that only the strongest, only the most hearty, and only the most capable can withstand a constant bombardment of their errors and still persevere. A more useful strategy is to interact with others as suggested by the lyrics sung by Bing Crosby: "Accentuate the positive, eliminate the negative." The language here is the language of acceptance, and of the behavior and attitude of the support parents and teachers can provide to each other. Encouragement is an effective method of helping parents and teachers gain feelings of acceptance and value. The use of encouragement requires that the teacher and the parent be honest with one another while at the same time being sensitive to the other's feelings. Encouragement is the language of acceptance because it is based on respect. Dinkmeyer, in his various programs, developed phrases that demonstrate acceptance from several different postures (Dinkmeyer & McKay, 1989; Dinkmeyer, McKay, & Dinkmeyer,1980). The following phrases show acceptance, confidence, appreciation, and recognition of effort:

Acceptance:
"I enjoy talking with you."
"I like the way you approach the problem."
"Since you are not pleased with your child's work, what do you think you could do help him or her to improve?"
Confidence:
"It shows you really thought through the problem."
"That's a difficult problem, but I believe you can work it out."
Appreciation:
"Thanks for your help with your child's homework."
"Thank you for helping Mary with her art."
"Thanks for tutoring Bill in math."
"Thank you for volunteering to work in the classroom."
Recognition of effort:
"You really worked hard on the volunteer project."
"Look at how much you have completed." (Try to be specific in reference to the amount.)
"You have really helped Sue improve her writing skills."

For parents and teachers to be encouraging of one another, they must be willing to value one another and to have faith in themselves.

Feeling cared for and cared about provides a reserve of support to carry a person through tough times. Spending time together is also encouraging.

Parent–Teacher Conferences

Many parents and teachers often dread this event. Parents and teachers may be afraid of being attacked, blamed, or asked to do something that might upset their daily routines. The focus may be lost because, ideally, parent-teacher conferences provide an opportunity to discuss the individual child. The goals of the parents and teachers are so closely related, but as is often the case in people who have high investments in others, the method to achieve those goals may differ. The sooner they are able to work together, the fewer the difficulties the child may have to overcome. The school counselor may choose a variety of formats to help parents and teacher connect to one another.

Skill-building workshops. These workshops for the entire staff can include brief discussions of how to have a successful conference, minidemonstrations by the counselor, and a chance for the participants to demonstrate their skills through role-playing. Role-playing allows teachers an opportunity to practice and apply their new skills in typical situations.

Teacher-parent-counselor conferences. These conferences allow counselors to model effective communication skills and to provide feedback to the teacher at relevant moments.

Parent Education

Efforts to increase parental awareness of effective child-rearing practices are not new. An increasing numbers of parents, dissatisfied with their child-rearing efforts, are expressing a need for information on how to improve familial relationships. It is important to help parents develop skills that will support their children's success and achievements. A highly effective parent education class is planned with the parents and school counselor. When the parents are involved in the planning, the counselor can be sure it is topical, relevant, and interesting to parents. The goal of parent education is to provide knowledge and skills to parents. Parents learn about child development, communication skills, and techniques for managing childhood behavior problems. Counselors also have a role in helping desperate parents and confused teenagers to revitalize their communication and maintain a bond to guide adolescents toward a more secure, autonomous adulthood. Most parents feel encouraged by sharing experiences and receiving support from other parents.

Pressures on the family to adjust to family development milestones (e.g., adolescence, independence, new schools) create a need for education in family living. Parents often express feelings of inadequacy in the family relationship. Some parents simply do not know what to do with their children. Traditional patterns of parental authority, under which a parent or teacher may have been raised, may no longer seem to work. Perhaps some parents have difficulty adjusting to new roles, such as becoming a stepparent.

Parent education and consultation are essential aspects of the school counselor's role. As the parents' attitudes toward their children and the school improves, the parent—it is hoped—will become more involved with the school. In selecting a parent education model, Bradley and Stone (1994) have suggested taking time to ensure the selected model will provide appropriate information to meet the needs of the parent and provide a philosophical foundation in meeting those needs. In selecting the appropriate model, consider such elements as parental reading level, education, and interest. Other factors such as cost, special training of the leaders, and availability of the materials should be considered.

A variety of approaches have been taken to parent education, using the following common reference terms: *parent support groups, parent study groups, single parent groups, stepfamily groups,* and *blended family groups.* Most formats include the presentation of specific ideas, group discussion, sharing of ideas and experiences, and skill-building activities. A typical parent education program consists of eight weekly workshop sessions, each lasting 90 minutes. The programs for parents with young children are designed to train parents in a behavioral method of child management. Parents are given instruction in observing and defining behaviors, recording behaviors, and applying consequences to behavior to increase, decrease, shape, or maintain these behaviors. Parents are instructed in methods of effective communication and participation in enjoyable activities to improve family relations.

These approaches share the same general objective: to assist parents who are attempting to change their method of interaction with their children for the purpose of encouraging positive behavior. Each of these approaches emphasizes the cognitive effort to reeducate parents. Behavioral programs focus primarily on modifying the observable behaviors of children and allowing parents to identify behaviors they want to encourage. The Adlerian approach, particularly Dinkmeyer and McKay's (1989) *Systematic Training for Effective Parenting* (STEP program), Bradley and Stone's (1994) *Parenting Without Hassles,* and Michael Popkin's (1993) *Active Parenting,* help parents understand the purpose of the child's behavior and learn techniques for encouraging their children toward responsible participation in the family. Thomas Gordon (1970), in *Parent Effectiveness Training,* described an approach in which parents are provided instruction to listen intently to their children and to communicate respect to the child. This approach is intended to produce a no-lose method of resolving conflicts.

Afterschool Parent-Led Enrichment Programs

Schools need to provide more opportunities for parent involvement and service. One method is to allow parents to provide afterschool enrichment programs. Many parents possess skills and strengths that they can contribute to enrichment programs. For example, parents can share stories that teach children to be safe, such as "Don't Talk to Strangers." This story, specifically, helps parents teach children to stay away from those who might abduct them; it might help decrease the number of children who turn up missing in the United States. For another example, a group of parents with limited English proficiency can become tutors and teach the Spanish language to students studying the language. Parents benefit from interaction with English-speaking students, and the school benefits from excellent resources. A cultural festival may provide an opportunity to interact with people from a variety of cultures. The festival might include a variety of foods, costumes, music, and dance. Programs in sewing, food preparation, crafts, carpentry, computers, and stress management also can help students who share a common interest. Creative scheduling will be necessary to allow parents to work afterschool hours, in evenings, on weekends, and during holidays. When parents are encouraged to volunteer on behalf of their children's school, several outcomes have been documented:

- Parents become more comfortable in interactions with the school staff.
- Students increase their learning skills and receive more individual attention.
- Students develop an ease of communication with adults.

- Teachers acquire an awareness of parent interest in school and children and parent willingness to help. (Sandell, 1998)

In planning any parent involvement program, it is important to consider the school setting. It may be necessary to provide transportation and child care for parents to attend school functions. It may also be necessary to plan conference dates and school activities far in advance to accommodate the busy schedules of parents. The most important consideration is that the school understands the community, its culture, and its needs so it can provide opportunities for parent involvement.

Parent involvement in education has been linked to higher achievement and many other positive outcomes for students and families. A variety of models are available that provide opportunities for parents to become involved in different ways in the children's education. Program models that are also good resources include the following.

The School Development Program. Funded by James Comer in 1968 in New Haven, Connecticut, the School Development Program (SDP) is based on the belief that the relationship between the school and the family is the critical factor in the education of children. The model emphasizes a comprehensive, collaborative, consensus-based, no-fault approach to problem solving. Teams of stakeholders create comprehensive school plans, including specific goals, assessment and modification, and staff development (Comer, 1993). Comer found that 1% to 5% of a school's parents are likely to be engaged as active decision makers; 10% to 25% are likely to serve as volunteers in schools; and 50% to 100% are likely simply to participate in parent–teacher conferences and social events.

Families Together With Schools. This program, formerly known as FAST: Families and Schools Together, was established in 1988 in Madison, Wisconsin, as a substance abuse prevention program in collaboration with elementary schools, mental health agencies, substance abuse prevention agencies, and families. The new name came into effect in 1993. The main goals are (1) to enhance family functioning by strengthening the parent and child relationship and by empowering parents as primary prevention agents for their own children; (2) to prevent the child from experiencing school failure by improving the child's behavior and performance in school, making parents partners in the educational process, and increasing the family's sense of affiliation with the school; and (3) to reduce stress experienced by parents and children in daily situations by developing support group for parents (McDonald, 1991).

Teachers Involve Parents in Schoolwork (TIPS). The TIPS program was developed by Epstein for the elementary grades at Johns Hopkins University in Baltimore, Maryland, in 1987. The program expanded to the middle grades in 1992 in collaboration with the Fund for Educational Excellence. The goals of the TIPS process are (1) to increase parent awareness of their children's schoolwork, (2) to increase parent involvement in their children's learning activities at home that are linked to class work, (3) to increase students' ability and willingness to talk about schoolwork at home and the frequency of this happening, and (4) to improve students' skills and homework completion in specific subjects (Epstein, 1993). The TIPS program establishes regular communication between the teacher and the parent or parents concerning language arts and science, health, and math. The homework is an interactive process that keeps families involved in their children's learning. The interactive activities require students to show, share, demonstrate, interview, gather reactions, and interact with the family. Suggestions for increasing parent–teacher communication that counselors can facilitate are included in the TIPS program. For example, the following tips for developing cooperative relationships between parents and teachers were distributed by the Parent Center, Albuquerque Public Schools, for teachers:

Getting off to a good start:

1. Make early contact.
2. Share special needs or concerns.
3. Clarify classroom program, expectations, and routine.
4. Honor time limitations.
5. Work on problem prevention.

Keeping communication flowing:

1. Maintain regular contact.
2. Plan for conferences.
3. Clarify understanding during conferences.
4. Listen.
5. Schedule follow-up.
6. Be supportive!
7. Include child in communication.
8. Verify information, if in doubt.
9. Problem-solve positively together.

Planning for another good year:

1. Summer activity recommendations.
2. Assistance in planning for next year.
3. Send a thank you.

Also for teachers, are these 10 ideas for including parents in their children's education:

1. Appeal to current volunteers and staff members to recruit their friends.
2. Find leaders from all communities, including typically underrepresented groups, and ask them to recruit their peers.
3. Be flexible in school meeting hours (i.e., early morning, late evening, weekend).
4. Host frequent curriculum or weekend enrichment courses for parents with make-it-take-it activities, parent work parties to make classroom material, mathematics night, and science fairs, hands-on computer time, and family writing conferences to record family stories.
5. Develop opportunities for parents to earn coupons or credits for their work at school; as coupons are accumulated, they are redeemable for prizes or services.
6. Encourage parents to share skills and expertise at school as a way of participating in the curriculum.
7. Organize afterschool, parent-led school enrichment programs.
8. Involve parents as volunteers to assist as tutors, teachers, assistants, door greeters, chaperones, typists, career mentors, and parent mentors.
9. Create opportunities for family volunteers to listen to students read, staff a computer laboratory, translate children's books, or share hobbies and collections.
10. Provide opportunities for parent education classes or workshops that focus on parent–child relationships.

Tips that counselors may choose to provide to parents to help in understanding their role in the education of their children are as follows:

1. Children regard the public presence of parents as a way of showing caring and connectedness.
2. Meaningful support should communicate to children that achievements are supported because they are good for children.

3. Emphasis should be on the child and not on achievement overload.
4. Parents should show support for the child with commitment in the amount of time and concern and not material support.
5. The parent is the teacher's partner in education, and parents and teachers can learn from and teach each other.

Tips that counselors may choose to provide to teachers to help in understanding how to improve parent/teacher communication are as follows:

1. Teachers need a better understanding of effective communication styles and skills to communicate with parents.
2. When empathy and warmth are used between parents and teachers, parents are likely to talk with teachers and seek their input when problems occur.
3. Understanding how teachers perceive parents and how parents perceive teachers helps understanding.
4. Teachers who realize how vulnerable and sensitive parents can be about their children have an easier time communicating with parents.
5. Sending home a note or making a telephone call that reveals the teacher's commitment to reaching the parent is an important step in connecting.

Conclusion

It is important for schools to seek parental support and involvement because this is vital for school counseling programs to be successful. Most parents agree that the growth and development of children is enhanced when parents and teachers work together effectively. Therefore, we can view the education as a partnership between parents and teachers. In any partnership, there is shared responsibility between parents and teachers for establishing and maintaining contact and communication. It is important that the school, teachers, and counselors form cooperative working relationships with parents in planning educational goals for their children. The relationships that counselors establish with teachers and parents have a tremendous impact on the choices children make regarding school performance, career decisions, friendships, and other developmental elements. Consulting with teachers and parents provides opportunities for parental support networks, better parent–teacher communication, and collaborative parent–teacher–counselor relationships. It is important that school counselors at all levels make every effort to establish good communication between parents and teachers, and to have parents involved in planning their children's educational goals. By forming a successful alliance between parents and teachers, counselors can encourage better parental involvement. This chapter has discussed ways for counselors to help improve the relationships between parents and teachers. Several practical suggestions for including parents and teachers have been provided, ranging from parent–teacher communication to parent education. When a collaborative relationship is established between parents and teachers, both are more willing to share concerns with each other. The major thrust of this chapter is to encourage the counselor to include the parents and teachers in a variety of school activities, to get to know one another. Children benefit when there is active and cooperative participation by parents, teachers, and counselors.

References

Ball, G. (1977). *Innerchange: A journey into self-learning through interaction.* La Mesa, CA: Human Development Training Institute.

Barr, R. D., & Parrett, W. H. (1995). *Hope at last for at-risk youth.* Boston: Allyn & Bacon.

Bradley, F. L., & Stone, L. A. (1994). *Parenting without hassles: Parents and children as partners.* Salem, WI: Sheffield.

Brammer, L. M. (1988). *The helping relationship: Process and skill* (4th ed.). Englewood Cliffs, NJ: Prentice Hall.

Comer, J. P. (1993). *School power: Implications of an intervention project.* New York: Free Press.

Dinkmeyer, D., & McKay, G. (1989). *Systematic training for effective parenting.* Circle Pines, MN: American Guidance Service.

Dinkmeyer, D., McKay, G., & Dinkmeyer, D. (1980). *Systematic training for effective teaching.* Circle Pines, MN: American Guidance Service.

Dreikurs, R., & Soltz, V. (1964). *Children: The challenge.* New York: Hawthorn.

Dustin, D., & Ehly, S. (1984). Skills for effective consultation. *The School Counselor, 32,* 23–39.

Epstein, J. L. (1993). School and family partnerships. *Instructor, 103*(2), 73–76.

Fuller, M. L. (1998). An introduction to families. In M. L. Fuller & G. Olsen (Eds.), *Home-school relations* (pp. 1–10). Needham Heights, MA: Allyn & Bacon.

Gordon, T. (1970). *P.E.T.: Parent effectiveness training.* New York: Wyden.

Hanhan, S. F. (1998). Parent-teacher communication: Who's talking? In M. L. Fuller & G. Olsen (Eds.), *Home-school relations* (pp. 106–126). Needham Heights, MA: Allyn & Bacon.

Henderson, A. T., & Berla, N. (1994). *A new generation of evidence: The family is critical to student achievement.* Columbia, MD: National Committee for Citizens in Education.

MacDonald, J. B. (1998). Teachers and parenting: Multiple views. In M. L. Fuller & G. Olsen (Eds.), *Home-school relations* (pp. 87–106). Needham Heights, MA: Allyn & Bacon.

McDonald, L. (1991). Families and schools together: An innovative substance abuse prevention program. *Social Work in Education, 13*(2), 118–128.

National Education Goals Panel. (1994). *The national education goals report: Building a nation of learners.* Washington, DC: U.S. Government Printing Office.

Popkin, M. H. (1993). *Active parenting today.* Atlanta, GA: Active Parenting.

Sandell, E. J. (1998). Parents in the schools. In M. L. Fuller & G. Olsen (Eds.), *Home-school relations* (pp.127–150). Needham Heights, MA: Allyn & Bacon.

Schmidt, J. J. (1999). *Counseling in schools.* Needham Heights, MA: Allyn & Bacon.

■ ■ ■

6

Working With Individual Children From a Family Systems Perspective

Lynn D. Miller, PhD

The reasons parents do not come to schools to participate in school functions and processes designed to help their child succeed are both psychological and practical.

The practical obstacles to participation include

lack of transportation,
lack of time in the workday,
inability to take time off from work,
competing commitments of other children,
lack of energy, and
lack of knowledge of problems.

The psychological obstacles to participation include

lack of interest,
avoidance of an institution where one does not feel welcome,
cultural value that discourages participation,
past poor history or poor relationship with school personnel,
defeatist attitude towards rebellious child, or "I give up!" syndrome.

Given this reality, school counselors need to work with children in some circumstances independent of their families while consistently reaching out to parents to become involved. How do counselors do this? This chapter first suggests several interventions to use with individual children, which taps into the child's family dynamics. These interventions are all low- or no-cost interventions, can be conducted in a limited amount of time, and can be used with individuals in a school counseling office or with a small group of children (five to six) in the school setting. The chapter then describes school-wide strategies that counselors can implement to shape the school system into a more positive, productive, and healthy environment for children. Finally, tips for increasing parental participation in schools are related.

Despite our best efforts to involve parents and families, and efforts to train our school staff in prevention and adaptive teaching techniques for behaviorally/emotionally difficult children, some children remain deeply troubled and will get no help other than what is provided by the school counselor, school social worker, school psychologist, or other mental health worker in the school. Indeed, estimates of children who suffer from serious emotional disorders range from 12% to 20%, but less than one third receive help (Estrada & Pinsof, 1995; National School Boards Association and American School Counselors Association, 1994). That makes more than two thirds of children who would qualify for help for mental disorders unlikely to receive treatment.

What are the most pervasive mental disorders in children? Surprisingly, many school personnel may erroneously guess it is attention deficit-hyperactivity disorder (ADHD), which enjoys a high profile in the press and demands attention from educators for behavioral disturbance, despite a prevalence rate of 3%–5%. Ironically, the two largest categories of childhood mental disturbance in the regular education population (special education students suffer from even higher rates of mental distress) are often overlooked precisely because the behavioral difficulties associated with them are more manageable in a large, public school classroom: anxiety, rate of prevalence 18%–22% (Dadds, Spence, Holland, Barrett, & Laurens, 1997; Muris, Merckelbach, Mayer, & Prins, 2000), and depression, rate of prevalence 2%–17% and diagnosed with increasing frequency as a child ages (Dubuque, 1998).

Therefore, nearly one quarter of the school population is suffering from mental distress, the vast majority from anxiety and depression. Why is it important to treat anxiety and depression early in life? Why not wait until adulthood for help? Depression and anxiety can have significant deleterious psychosocial effects during adolescence and, if left untreated, can lead to poor functioning during young adulthood. These effects range from more severe depressive episodes, substance abuse, lower rates of college completion, lower income levels, and increased likelihood of becoming a single parent (Lewinsohn & Clarke, 1999). Of course the worst outcome for untreated depression is suicide. Suicide is the third leading cause of death among 15- to 24-year-olds (in Canada and the United States) and is thought to be on the increase (National Center for Health Statistics, 1998).

So does counseling and therapy with children affect these rates of anxiety and depression? A meta-analysis (i.e., synthesis of studies for larger comparative purpose) of six outcome studies using cognitive-behavioral approaches reported an overall effect size of –1.27 (expresses mean differences between studies in standard deviation units), and 63% of the children showed clinically significant improvement at the end of treatment (Lewinsohn & Clarke, 1999). Although treatments vary, a cognitive behavioral approach is seemingly the preferred method that can be conducted in a classroom or school counseling setting.

What about environmental influences? Numerous studies support the finding that psychosocial adjustment of children is directly related to parenting style and communication (Patterson, 1986; Rapee, 1997; Steinberg, 1987). For example, adolescents who regularly engage in at-risk behavior are more likely to come from families with inept parenting styles. Likewise, children from homes in which positive and democratic parenting styles are in use are some of the most well adjusted. If parents will not come into the school for family counseling, it may be consistent with a laissez faire parenting style. The school counselor may be able to effect change with a child in an individual approach. What is clear, regardless of the parenting style, is that these children need individual attention and one-to-one counseling.

Specific Strategies for Working With Individual Children From a Family Perspective

What can school counselors and the school system provide for the emotional wellness of these and other children? The strategies in this section can be used with individual children to gain a broader understanding of the family network, to encourage strengths, and to help the child make sense of his or her environment. Traditionally, a school counselor may focus on academic success, social skill training, reduction in peer conflict, and so on. These strategies are based on the presumption that a child acts out at school because of underlying stress from conflict or struggles at home with family members. If the child can gain insight into the dysfunction at home, be acknowledged for these difficulties in a trusting and safe environment, express frustration or other emotion, and then be offered explanation, alternative social responses, or coping strategies, the child may understand the source of stress and perhaps feel more in control.

Play Therapy Techniques

Play therapy can be incorporated into all counseling approaches and can be useful for all ages. Play is an integral part of children's lives, provides a venue for communication between those who have limited cognitive development and those trying to help, and is a natural mode of learning and relating to others (Landreth, 1982). Indeed, Landreth stated that play therapy is an essential tool for every school counselor. School counselors should seek opportunities to be trained in play therapy techniques in recognition of the impressive therapeutic benefits to children and families. A counselor should assume that play therapy is useful with older children: Children of all ages benefit from play therapy intervention.

Children can express their thoughts and feelings, likes and dislikes, and hopes and fears through play. Decisions can be made without fear of failure, humiliation, or sanctions. Positive and negative feelings can be expressed and pent-up emotions can be released through play rather than by talking. New solutions to old problems can be discovered and integrated into new behaviors. This control and mastery contributes to a child's development and self-confidence.

A counselor can explore the family hierarchy, family constellation, and family interactional patterns through any of several techniques. This focus on family dynamics allows the child to explore needs and feelings that are unmet and unexpressed in his or her daily life. Erikson (1950) believed that children attempt to understand the rules and regulations of the adult world through their play. Through this discovery, children become more aware of what they feel, who they are and what they need, and realize they can make choices about their behaviors and attitudes. The counselor can review recurrent themes (e.g., violence, loss of power, inconsistent rules and roles) and offer suggestions to the child for coping at home and gaining insight into behavior at school. Classroom teachers, an adult mentor, the counseling staff, or other school personnel can then offer modifications and support.

Family drawings. The Kinetic Family drawing technique directs the child to draw his or her family doing something. This is a projective technique that is interpreted as a reflection of how the child thinks and feels about his or her family. Ask the child to draw Dad's house and to draw Mom's house. This begins a conversation of different expectations for living in or visiting two households during a divorce, separation, or remarriage. Ask the child to draw the way the family is now and how the family could be. This allows the counselor to help the child contribute to changes that can be made to a home situation and to accept (and learn to adapt to) those that cannot be made.

Family clay figures or assignment of action heroes to family members. This technique allows the child to gain distance from an emotional situation and represent family members with inanimate objects. The counselor can normalize behaviors or help the child to understand the stress and conflict under which he or she lives.

Paper bag puppets and enactment of family situations using the puppets. Children can decorate paper bags with magic markers, felt, and construction paper to represent family members (one bag for each significant family member). These paper bags then can be used as puppets (child slips hand into each paper bag to make it "talk") to recreate conversations at home or to practice new social skills with the guidance of the counselor.

Internalized Other

This is an interviewing process created by Karl Tomm (1998). According to Tomm, an internalized community, which includes all the individuals with whom a person has been in a relationship or has even only heard about, constitutes each of us. The counselor interviews another person (e.g., parent, teacher, sibling) within the self (i.e., the child) as a method for helping the child get in touch with experiences of the other. An interview may go like this:

Counselor: I would like to ask you a few questions, Leon, as if you were actually your stepfather. I want you to answer these from your inside picture of him. Say what you feel might be going on inside your stepdad, and even say the things he might not say but that you think or expect he might say or feel.

Leon: OK.

Counselor: (To Leon): Let me start by talking to you as "Bud" and ask you, Bud, how do you feel about coming to the high school and talking to the school counselor today?

Leon: Well, I'm kind of mad because I had to get off of work early.

Counselor: Well, Bud, I sure am glad that you are here because it sends a clear message to your stepson, Leon, that he is important to you.

Leon: Well, I guess he is kind of important, but I never tell him that.

Counselor: Bud, I think that it is difficult to tell our children how important they are to us, but I bet you show Leon lots of ways that he is important. Can you tell me some things you do that let him know?

Leon: Oh, maybe that I married his mom and knew that I was going to be a stepdad, even though I don't really like kids that much. And I work long hours at a job that I hate.

This allows the counselor to see what is disturbing Leon, and it gives Leon a chance to reflect on the behavior of someone close to him. Tomm stated there are many possible effects of this kind of interviewing, but one of the more significant ones allows the child to become more fully aware of the actual effects he or she may be having on the experience of someone else.

Psychodrama

Psychodrama allows a person to enact his or her problem, instead of just talking about it (Knittel, 1990). The advantage of psychodrama is that it converts the participant's urge toward acting out (a psychological defense mechanism) into the constructive channel of acting in, which leads to insight. A child can be encouraged to act like every person in his or her family: stand, sit, talk, walk, and so on, as if he or she were that person. More typically a psychodrama is enacted with others and should only be encouraged when group members are well acquainted with each other. In this case, a psychodrama should include the following:

- The child picks out a concrete example of a problem, one that can be enacted.
- The child chooses other students in the group who represent members of the child's social group (i.e., family).

- The counselor helps the other participants play their roles with feedback from the child.
- Future plans, hopes, and fears can be symbolically realized and explored, or guilt, resentments, and yearnings can be expressed.
- The counselor helps the child develop adaptive attitudinal and behavioral responses. (Blatner, 1973)

Role-Plays

Role-playing allows the child to practice a conversation with a parent that is weighing heavily on the child's mind. The counselor can play the part of the parent, or sometimes a more effective role-play is when the counselor plays the part of the student, and the student plays the part of the parent (reverse role-play). Both situations allow the counselor to make suggestions for talking to the parent in a nonconflictual setting, express appropriate phrasing of concern, define a goal of the conversation, and explore expectations of the student.

Goals of Behavior and Misbehavior

Often a brief psychoeducational discussion with a student regarding Dreikurs and Soltz's (1964) ideas of the goals of misbehavior (attention, power, revenge, or display of inadequacy) allows insight into problems and can help alleviate stress and anxiety. For instance, if a student is troubled by a younger sibling's misbehavior, the counselor can have frank discussions with the student discussing that most children misbehave for a purpose. Children often use behavior to communicate their dislike for the way things are going at home. Enlisting the student's support and ideas about how to meet these mistaken or negative goals of a sibling fosters a sense of competence and empowerment. It can also encourage the development of empathy. For some mature students, it can shed insight into their own behavior, and may lead to a frank discussion of alternate, more effective approaches to reaching a desired goal.

Contracting

Contracting, which establishes goals, outcomes, consequences, and rewards, makes action planning concrete for children. This can reduce the tendency to blame others for failure of the student to act, increase student responsibility, and highlight the need for individuals to be problem solvers. The key to contracting is to make the consequences logical (i.e., have the consequence fit the failure of the activity) and rewards appealing and obtainable. Another key to successful contracting is to make sure the goals are what the counselee wants and not necessarily exclusively what the school system wants. Successful attainment should be measured in small increments, rather than large, overwhelming steps.

A contract should be discussed, at least over the phone, with the adult in the home. Commitment should be made to reinforce the contract at home. The contract should take a prominent place in the home, (e.g., be taped to the refrigerator). If the family is not involved in either the reward or consequences of the contract, one person in the school should be assigned to follow up with the student, as in a parental role.

Dollhouse

Similar to other enactment environments, a dollhouse allows the child to express his or her feelings about the home and allows the counselor to envision the home life. One example of the use of a dollhouse with a middle-school boy was that after joking with the boy that dollhouses were fun places to play, the teen revealed that he was sleeping on top of the freezer that was located in the basement. This discovery allowed the counselor to contact a social service agency that supplied essential furniture for low-income families, which delivered a more suitable bed for the student. Often big-box retailers (e.g., K-mart, Wal-Mart) donate slightly damaged goods, such as a dollhouse, upon request to those in need of training materials or to nonprofit groups.

Storytelling

Many people listen better to stories than lectures, and children can become engrossed in a story in which they play a main part. Storytelling helps a child talk about the painful events that are difficult to talk about, even though talking is a great healing method. Loss, either through death or divorce, is a particularly difficult topic for most people or can be more traumatic for children and teens because they are often overlooked in the grieving process. Storytelling can help eliminate some of the questions most often pondered by children.

For instance, one school counselor conducted a group session on grief and loss and used the metaphor of a "choo-choo" train with early elementary students. Each child had a chance to drive the train (made up of all the group members seated in chairs in a line) to that safe, happy place where the deceased person was, and all the members added their thoughts as to what they thought was there.

Violet Oaklander (1978) also described the use of storytelling as a way of increasing the child's self-awareness and cited fantasy and imagery, such as the wise-person fantasy, as good ways to tap intuitive thought in children and adults.

Sand Play

Sand often acts as a magnet for children. "When miniature toys are added, a whole world appears, dramas unfold, and absorption is total. The child has the opportunity to resolve the traumas by externalizing the fantasies and developing a sense of mastery and control over inner impulses" (Allan & Berry, 1987, p. 300).

This allows the child to develop a story in a nonthreatening fashion, with characters, toys, or objects representing family members. This enables the student to convey his or her own theme, if listened to by a trained ear. When the theme makes sense to the player, sometimes there are clues expressed that can shed light for solving an ongoing problem (Leben, 1994).

Developing Resilience in the School Environment

The school counselor also has a larger system at his or her disposal: the school system. Although the family may be disenfranchised or uninterested in family counseling at the school site, the counselor can rely on the larger net of the school environment to establish a healthy environment for the troubled child. This is a systems approach. Researchers have hypothesized that many children, despite the plethora of problems in their home environment, are resilient to these negative home effects because of a character trait called *resiliency*. The development and encouragement of resiliency in children promises to mitigate the effects of disenfranchised parents, neglect, and poor parenting. Warner in Henderson and Milstein (1996) discussed resilience and sustained competence in relation to positive developmental outcomes among children who live in high-risk contexts, such as chronic poverty or parental substance abuse, prolonged stress, and trauma or violent environments. For those children who develop successfully, specific protective conditions seem to serve as buffers and are determinants of resiliency development (Garmezy, 1985).

Effective school research (Good & Brophy, 1986) has confirmed that some schools are more successful than others in producing higher achieving students because of similar school environmental characteristics. For instance, a school that is characterized by shared values and a shared educational culture is more successful. These values include a strong sense of community, high expectations for students, a moral order that entails respect for authority, a genuine and pervasive caring about individuals, respect for people's feelings and attitudes, mutual trust, and the consistent enforcement of norms that define and delimit acceptable behavior.

How do schools do this? Effective schools are more likely to produce resilient children. The school environment is a critical variable and context for children's development of resilient attitudes and behaviors. The school counselor, with administrative support, can train, teach, and foster these elements in school staff as part of professional development in-services and as part of teacher consultation.

School-Wide Strategies

Henderson and Milstein (1996) have outlined six strategies for fostering resiliency in schools:

Set clear and consistent boundaries. Classroom, school, and playground rules, policies, and procedures should be clearly written, communicated, and paired with appropriate consequences that are consistently enforced. Anxiety is often a result of not knowing what to expect and feeling a loss of control. People therefore do better under circumstances of structure, expectations, and clear boundaries. Children especially need to be trained in routine. Children from chaotic homes particularly thrive given clear expectations, limits, and consequences.

Practical implementation. An attitude of caring rather than punishment should be the foundation of these boundaries. It is crucial that staff, students, and the available (and willing) parents are all involved in writing these expectations and communicating the results in poster form throughout the building as well as via letters home. These policies can be restated in classrooms, at assemblies, in slogans, and in the lunchroom, and reinforced throughout the day and school year.

Increase prosocial bonding via a mentoring program. This strategy aims to strengthen the positive connections that children form. Individuals are encouraged to bond students to school and academic accomplishments. This can be an adult-child pairing from the community in a mentor program, or it can be a relationship that is encouraged within the school setting, such as a pairing with a custodian, secretary, lunch person, bus driver, crossing guard, or physical education teacher.

Practical implementation. Students need to be encouraged to participate in a variety of activities in, before, and after school. These activities will help them bond with one another as well as foster an interest in the arts, drama, music, sports, community service, and clubs of all types. More companies are encouraging employees to become mentors as they adopt particular schools.

Run groups that teach life skills. School counselors need to be running small and large groups that teach the skills of cooperation, conflict resolution, assertiveness training, communication skills, problem solving and decision making, and healthy stress management. If these skills are taught and reinforced at a young age, the difficulties of adolescence, including use of alcohol and drugs and sexual interactions, are lessened (Resnick et al., 1997). These skills also assist in creating a conducive learning environment and help foster effective interactions with adults in the school building. Research has demonstrated that peers are the best messengers of prevention and intervention strategies, so it is useful to identify all the ways students can help teach life skills to one another.

Practical implementation. Counselors need to be running groups consistently throughout the year. Working with a different group (6–7 children) for 40 minutes at lunch every day (5 days per week) for 6 weeks throughout the year (36-week school term) allows a counselor to establish relationships with 195 children (6–7 children x 5 days x 6 group cycles). This is time efficient.

Focus on school climate. Provide caring and support. This dimension includes Rogers's concept of unconditional positive regard and Adler's use of encouragement. Henderson and Milstein (1996) considered a healthy school environment the most critical of all the elements that promote resiliency. This is a school climate issue that begins in the front office and can be found throughout the fabric of the school. Respect should be demonstrated by all to all. School counselors can facilitate teacher collaboration, team building, and conflict management.

Practical implementation. Respect can be demonstrated by knowing and calling students by their names, involving those who may be reluctant to participate, catching students doing something kind, and organizing assemblies that promote recognition of those who demonstrate caring and support. Pair older children with younger children or pair student volunteers with children with special needs.

Set and communicate high expectations. Expectations for all students need to be both high and realistic to be effective motivators. This can be a frustrating component in that many at-risk children have been labeled and subsequently adopt low expectations for themselves, leading to a "learned helplessness" (Seligman, 1981), which can actually promote depression. Students should be told regularly that they can succeed and that the adults in the building will not give up on them. Curriculum, instruction, and assessment of student learning should be based on clearly defined and important student outcomes. A focus should be on preferred learning style.

Practical implementation. Classrooms should embody high expectations by promoting higher order, more meaningful, and participatory curricula; grouping students heterogeneously, according to interest, and with flexibility; and evaluating in ways that recognize multiple intelligence and learning styles.

Provide opportunities for meaningful participation. This strategy means giving students much of the responsibility for what goes on in school. Resiliency develops when people are actively engaged in making meaningful decisions about how the school operates and where, what, and when they learn. This needs to be negotiated in a climate that demonstrates responsibility for academic standards. Students should be on all committees and given responsibility for committee work. People support what they help to create.

Practical implementation. Students are the greatest resource schools have, yet they are often viewed as passive objects or problems or are completely forgotten. Students should be given every feasible opportunity to participate in the day-to-day chores of the school (e.g., picking up attendance slips, helping in the gym, answering phones, filing) as well as in special events (e.g., student representative on committees, participation in decoration and running of school dances).

Tips for Increasing Parental Participation

Many counselors have been frustrated by their attempts to involve parents in school activities that met with little response. Often this leads to the false conclusion that parents do not care or, worse, must not love their children. In fact, most parents do care about their children and want to be involved, informed, and feel competent and respected. A 1993 study surveyed 1,188 African American and Latino parents; 97% of respondents stated that they wanted to be more involved with their children's education, from helping with homework to having more influence at the school (Chavkin, 1993). However, in another study, the U.S. Office of Educational Research and Improvement (Powell, 1990) discovered that only 50% of parents had attended a school meeting since the beginning of the school year. This is a large discrepancy. We can conclude that positive intentions of parents to be involved exist, but the intentions are not often acted upon. Perhaps schools as a whole need to look at the barriers to involvement and misconceptions surrounding reluctant parents.

What Are the Barriers to Involvement?

Parental involvement may be a key to educational opportunity. Toomey (1992) suggested that parents who come to school—or enthusiasts as they are seen by school staff—have children who are in turn favored in the system. These same parents are more likely to feel comfortable and confident in the school setting and model more commitment to the educational program. This feeds the positive cycle of reinforcement for these children. Educators need to identify what inhibits some parents from becoming involved and becoming enthusiasts. Inhibiting factors may include the following:

- Scheduled events may be at inconvenient times for working or single parents.
- Child care for other children may be impossible.
- Perceived lack of relevancy, power, or voice in school meetings may discourage parents.
- The cultural assumption by educators that education is not held in high regard by families discourages families from contributing.
- Transportation to the school may be burdensome.
- Negative past experience working with school or teacher might discourage parents.
- A youthful parent who may be a school dropout might harbor a poor attitude.
- Maslow's hierarchy of needs takes precedence: Food, shelter, and clothing may presuppose additional efforts at schools.

- Discrimination or lack of cultural sensitivity may discourage many parents.
- Simple lack of understanding of how to help their own child and lack of confidence to ask for help can prevent parents from contributing. (White-Clark & Decker, 1994)

What Can Schools Do to Be More Inviting?

Schools can take specific actions to encourage parent involvement. For example, they can

- partner families with other families in school community. Similar to pairing children with adult mentors, families can benefit from being paired with other veteran families;
- be flexible in school meeting hours (e.g., early morning, late evening, weekend conferencing);
- consider home visits at the convenience of families;
- access someone powerful in the hard-to-reach family's circle (e.g., employer, neighbor, religious community) to collaborate with school;
- be vigilant that school-to-home communication uses appropriate language (translations included) and appropriate reading levels, provides jargon-free information, encourages reciprocal communication instead of one-way communication, and includes practical quick tips for parents to use in homework help, hygiene, development, friendship, communication skills, and family rituals;
- recognize that parents have important, different, expert perspectives of their children;
- be proactive, rather than reactive. Telephone home to all children's families, emphasizing strengths;
- approach families individually, persuasively, and unconditionally; and
- focus on what works, rather than what doesn't, which sets a tone of solution building rather than pathology hunting.

Conclusion

Schools generally seek parental support and involvement in the school system. Support ranges from being classroom helpers to attendance monitors to a member of a site-based management team. However, many parents remain uninvolved in their child's school life, often to the detriment of their child's success (the exceptions to this are those families highly involved with the school and the administrative team in a disciplinary mode). School counselors understand the ubiquitous influence of the family on a child and can work from a family systems perspective with individual children, without other family members actually present in the counseling session.

Several practical suggestions for enabling children to understand their own families are detailed, ranging from play therapy techniques to sand play. A child needs to understand and be acknowledged for having accurate upsetting feelings that may emanate from a chaotic or stressful home environment. When a child feels safe emotionally and mentally, he or she is liberated to concentrate on academic concerns. The school environment itself can be ameliorated to provide a caring, healthy environment in which respect is modeled and taught throughout the building. Safe, happy, respectful schools produce resilient children.

References

Allan, J., & Berry, P. (1987). Sandplay. *Elementary School Guidance and Counseling, 21*, 300–306.

Blatner, H. (1973). *Acting-in.* New York: Springer.

Chavkin, N. F. (1993). *Families and schools in a pluralistic society.* Albany: State University of New York Press.

Dadds, M. R., Spence, S. H., Holland, D. E., Barrett, P. M., & Laurens, K. R. (1997). Prevention and early intervention for anxiety disorders: A controlled trial. *Journal of Consulting and Clinical Psychology, 65*(4), 627–635.

Dreikurs, R., & Soltz, V. (1964). *Children: The challenge.* New York: Hawthorn.

Dubuque, S. E. (1998). Fighting childhood depression. *The Education Digest, 63*, 65–69.

Erikson, E. (1950). *Childhood and society.* New York: Norton.

Estrada, A. U., & Pinsof, W. M. (1995). The effectiveness of family therapies for selected behavioral disorders of childhood. *Journal of Marital and Family Therapy, 21*, 403–440.

Garmezy, N. (1985). Stress resistant children: The search for protective factors. In J. E. Stevenson (Ed.), *Recent research in developmental psychopathology* (pp. 213–33). New York: Elsevier.

Good, T. L., & Brophy, J. E. (1986). School effects. In M. C. Wittrock (Ed.), *The handbook of research on teaching* (3rd ed., pp. 570–604). New York: Macmillan.

Henderson,.N., & Milstein, M. M. (1996). *Resiliency in schools: Making it happen for students and educators.* Thousand Oaks, CA: Corwin Press.

Knittel, M. (1990). Strategies for directing psychodrama with the adolescent. *Journal of Group Psychotherapy, Psychodrama, and Sociometry, 43*(3), 116–120.

Landreth, G. (Ed.). (1982). *Play therapy: Dynamics of the process of counseling with children.* Springfield, IL: Charles C Thomas.

Leben, N. Y. (1994). *Directive group play therapy—60 structured games for the treatment of ADHD, low self-esteem, and traumatized children.* Pflugerville, TX: Morning Glory Treatment Center for Children.

Lewinsohn, P. M., & Clarke, G. N. (1999). Psychosocial treatments for adolescent depression. *Clinical Psychology Review, 19*(3), 329–342.

Muris, P., Merckelbach, H., Mayer, B., & Prins, E. (2000). How serious are common childhood fears? *Behaviour Research and Therapy, 38,* 217–228.

National Center for Health Statistics. (1998, May 28). *FASTATS A to Z.* Retrieved May 28, 1998, from http://www.cdc.gov/nchswww/fastats/suicide/htm

National School Boards Association and American School Counselors Association. (1994). *Caring connections: Helping young people from troubled homes.* St. Louis, MO: Author.

Oaklander, V. (1978). *Windows to our children.* Moab, UT: Real People Press.

Patterson, G. R. (1986). Performance models for antisocial boys. *American Psychologist, 41,* 432–444.

Powell, D. R. (1990). *Parent education and support programs.* Washington, DC: U.S. Office of Educational Research and Improvement. (ERIC Document Reproduction Service No. ED320661)

Rapee, R. M. (1997). Potential role of childrearing practices in the development of anxiety and depression. *Clinical Psychology Review, 17*(1), 47–67.

Resnick, M. D., Bearman, P. S., Blum, R. W., Bauman, K. E., Harris, K. M., Jones, J., et al. (1997). Protecting adolescents from harm: Findings from the national longitudinal study on adolescent health. *Journal of the American Medical Association, 278,* 823–832.

Seligman, M.E.P. (1981). A learned helplessness point of view. In L. P. Rehm (Ed.), *Behavior therapy for depression* (pp. 123–141). New York: Academic Press.

Steinberg, L. (1987). Single parents, step-parents, and the susceptibility of adolescents to antisocial pressure. *Child Development, 58,* 269–275.

Tomm, K. (1998). Social constructionist/narrative couple therapy. In T. Maccormack & K. Tomm (Eds.), *Case studies in couple and family therapy* (pp. 303–330). New York: Guilford Press.

Toomey, D. (1992, April). *Short-and medium-run effects of parents reading to preschool children in a disadvantaged locality.* Paper presented at the annual meeting of the American Educational Research Association, San Francisco. (Eric Document Reproduction Service No. ED346439)

White-Clark, R., & Decker, L. E. (1994). *The "hard-to-reach" parent: Old challenges, new insights.* National Community Education Publication Series.

■ ■ ■

PART

III

OUTCOME
RESEARCH
IMPLICATIONS

7

Research: What Works in Schools

Susan C. Whiston, PhD,
and Carla M. Teed, MA

Outcome research can serve as an important information source for school counselors because this type of research examines counseling practice. The typical format of outcome research involves providing a counseling intervention, then measuring the outcome or effectiveness of the intervention. Whiston and Sexton (1998) argued that it was important for school counselors to become knowledgeable about outcome research, so they could provide effective services to students. Lambert (1991) contended that without a thorough knowledge of the counseling outcome research, a practitioner cannot ethically counsel. He argued that counselors are ethically bound to provide the best services to their clients, and without thorough knowledge of the research, they will not know what has been shown to be the best practices. Moreover, administrators, teachers, parents, and community members are more likely to be supportive of school counseling activities that have been shown to be effective. In both counseling and psychotherapy, there is a movement toward research-based interventions and empirically supported treatments (Wampold, Lichtenberg, & Waehler, in press). This same trend is also evident in education, where teachers are encouraged to use instructional programs that are supported by research (Evensen & Hmelo, 2000; National Reading Panel, 2000). In the current era of accountability in education, it is anticipated that there will be demands for evidence that shows school counselors have a positive influence on students. Thus, knowledge of school counseling research can assist counselors in implementing effective services within their own schools and can be useful in informing other individuals about the benefits of school counseling. This chapter is designed to examine school counseling outcome research and describe which school-based interventions are supported empirically.

School Counseling Research

In examining the research concerning the effectiveness of school counseling interventions, it is important to consider the amount and quality of the research that has examined whether school counselors have a positive effect. We cannot rely on the results of one study to document the effectiveness of school counseling because there are limitations within most research designs and methodologies. Furthermore, administrators, school board members, and parents are often skeptical about instituting programs and counseling activities for which there is limited research. There is a need for more outcome research in school counseling because there is neither the quantity nor quality of studies in school counseling research that there is in other areas of counseling (Sexton, 1996). There is a particular need for research related to outcomes of comprehensive school counseling programs that claim to assist students in their academic, career, and personal/social development because little research has examined the effects of these guidance programs (Perry, 1993). In a review of school counseling outcome research, Whiston and Sexton (1998) found there was sufficient research from which to draw conclusions about certain aspects of school counseling but that many of the activities typically engaged in by school counselors had not been adequately studied. Although there is a clear need for additional school counseling research, this discussion identifies those aspects of school counseling for which there is sufficient research to warrant conclusions about efficacy and to identify those school counseling activities for which more research is needed before conclusions can be made.

Empirically Supported Interventions

The school counseling outcome research does appear to support school counselors being involved in individual and group counseling activities. Wiggins and Moody (1987) compared the counseling programs of schools that were evaluated by students and a team of evaluators as being highly effective, average, or below average. This study found that counselors in the highly effective programs spent more than 70% of their time in direct services (i.e., individual and group counseling activities) and very little time doing clerical activities. Prout and Prout (1998) found school-based group interventions had an average effect size of .97, which indicates these interventions are highly effective. Whiston and Sexton (1998) found that there was substantial support for group approaches for social skills training, family adjustment issues, and discipline problems. An early meta-analysis of prevention interventions found that therapeutic activities that promoted communication skills and deliberate psychological education tend to be effective (Baker, Swisher, Nadenickek, & Popowicz, 1984). In addition, the results from other studies indicated relaxation groups and cognitive-behavioral approaches to group counseling are effective (Bauer, Sapp, & Johnson, 2000; Kiselica, Baker, Thomas, & Reddy, 1994; Prout & Prout, 1998). School counselors, however, should be aware that the majority of research on group counseling in schools has been conducted primarily with younger students, and further study of the effectiveness of group approaches with high school students is needed.

Another area where there does appear to be compelling support is career counseling and guidance. There is support for career counseling with clients at various developmental levels, from both narrative reviews (Myers, 1986; Swanson, 1995) and meta-analyses (Oliver & Spokane, 1988; Whiston, Sexton, & Lasoff, 1998). These two meta-analyses found that career interventions were moderately to highly effective, depending on the types of interventions provided. In addition, these meta-analyses indicated that individual career counseling and career classes were the most effective methods of providing assistance in career development. Concerning career interventions specifically in school settings, Baker and Taylor (1998) found that career education activities designed to assist students in school-to-work transitions also had a moderate effect size. Whiston and Sexton (1998) also supported the effectiveness of career interventions in a school setting. They found career counseling activities seemed to assist a wide range of students (i.e., minority, learning disabled, and gifted students).

Lapan, Gysbers, and Sun (1997) compared schools with more fully implemented guidance programs to schools with a less programmatic approach. The students from schools with more fully implemented programs were more likely to report (a) they had earned higher grades; (b) their education better prepared them for the future; (c) they had more career and college information available to them; and (d) their schools had a more positive environment. Another study (Gysbers, Lapan, & Blair, 1999), found that school counselors who had more fully implemented guidance programs rated their programs as having higher levels of engagement and more visibility in the community. In addition, although the results were somewhat mixed, those schools with more fully implemented guidance programs reported a reduction in the performance of nonguidance tasks.

There is growing empirical support for the effectiveness of consultation as an indirect method of providing psychologically oriented services (Gutkin & Curtis, 1990; Zins, 1993). School counselors are often involved in consultation activities with parents, teachers, and other educational professionals. Gerler (1985) concluded that consultation with teachers was an effective method of influencing elementary school children's behavior. Furthermore, Borders and Drury (1992) found consultation activities to be effective at both the elementary and secondary levels. A secondary benefit to consultation activities may be increased referrals: Otwell and Mullis (1997) found that a consultation workshop held with teachers resulted in more students being referred for counseling. In terms of skills that increase the effectiveness of consultation, Gresham and Kendell (1987) found problem identification to be the most important process variable. Zins (1993) found a direct approach to be most effective in enhancing consultees' problem-solving skills. He recommended that counselors directly train consultees in problem-solving, communications, and intervention techniques. He further recommended that counselors overtly model for their consultees the problem-solving process.

Mixed or Insufficient Research

Although there are some school counseling activities for which there is empirical support, there are other important areas where the research results are not consistently positive or there has not been sufficient inquiry from which to draw conclusions. For example, school counselors are increasingly being asked to perform guidance curriculum activities (Gysbers & Henderson, 2000), but there has been surprisingly little research evaluating the effectiveness of those interventions. Whiston and Sexton (1998) were unable to identify any clear research trends concerning classroom guidance activities at the middle school and high school levels because of the limited number of studies conducted with these two age groups. Whiston and Sexton (1998) did, however, identify some trends at the elementary level. They found five studies related to the influence of classroom guidance activities on self-esteem or self-concept of elementary students. The results of the studies are, at best, mixed and not particularly supportive of the effects of classroom guidance activities on measures of self-esteem. Of these five studies, the results from two studies indicated that certain guidance curriculum activities designed to increase self-esteem had a positive influence on academic achievement. Given the current focus on accountability in education, school counselors may want to encourage the further exploration of the relationship between guidance curriculum activities and educational attainment.

There is no empirical support for the efficacy of clerical and paperwork activities. Wiggins and Moody (1987) found that in school counseling programs that were rated as below average, counselors spent between 24% and 43% of their time performing clerical tasks. Moreover, the researchers found that the counselors who were spending their time disproportionately performing clerical activities were not always forced to do so by their administrators. The counselors in these below-average schools did not have organized school counseling programs nor were the majority of these counselors knowledgeable about implementing needs assessments and using such results for programmatic planning. Other research has found that parents, students, and teachers felt that the least important activities for school counselors involved paperwork, clerical tasks, and coordinating testing programs (Schmidt, 1995).

There appears to be an increasing interest in peer mediation programs, which is reflected in Shepard's (1994) finding that since 1991 conflict resolution programs in the schools have increased by 40%. Some of the reviews of research in this area indicated that there was empirical support for peer counseling and peer mediation programs at both the elementary and secondary levels (Borders & Drury, 1992; Whiston & Sexton, 1998). Lewis and Lewis (1996) found, however, that many of these peer helping programs were supervised by noncounseling professionals and questioned whether these individuals had the proper training to supervise these peer helping programs. This concern was legitimized when they found in a later study (Lewis & Lewis, 1999) that those schools with noncounselors supervising the peer helping programs had higher suicide rates than schools where a professional school counselor supervised the peer program. They further analyzed the effectiveness of peer mediation and counseling programs and concluded that the tenuous findings in this area did not support the widespread usage of peer mediation programs.

Lately, sophisticated data analyses techniques have contributed to a growing body of literature related to implementing effective school-based drug prevention programs (Tobler, 1994). Tobler and Stratton (1997) found that, in general, drug prevention programs were only slightly effective; however, the effectiveness of the programs increased if the delivery method was interactive as compared with noninteractive methods. Programs, such as Project DARE (Drug Awareness Resistance Education), that rely primarily on information dissemination and lecture format were less effective than programs that focused more on group process and student participation. Research in this area indicates that students need to be actively involved and participate in the drug prevention programs for these programs to have an influence on later drug usage.

Family-Related Interventions

Unlike the school counseling literature that has limited empirical support, the area of family counseling has a rich and substantial history of empirical inquiry (Sexton & Alexander, in press). Many professionals have argued that family interventions and counseling fall under the responsibilities of school counselors (Kraus, 1998; Lewis, 1996). In the last 20 years of the *Elementary School Guidance and Counseling* journal, 21 articles were published related to family issues and counseling (Schmidt, Lanier, & Cope, 1999). In examining the research related to family interventions, three areas appear that are particularly pertinent to school counseling: divorce or family transition interventions, parent education, and family therapy.

Divorce or Family Transition Interventions

School counseling services need to be responsive to the needs of families in transition and students dealing with issues surrounding their parents' divorce. Children of divorce experience a significant upset in their family system, which can result in a number of adverse effects (Cantrell, 1986). Guidubaldi, Cleminshaw, Perry, and Mcloughlin (1983) reported that children of divorce are at risk for problems in school. They found that children of divorce had more disruptive classroom behavior, were absent more, and were more likely to repeat a grade than children from intact homes. Likewise,

Bisnaire, Firestone, and Rynard (1990) found that 30% of their sample had decreased academic performance following parental separation. Family involvement and family–school collaboration is slowly emerging in state and federal legislation to enhance student development by considering all environmental influences in the ecosystem of the child and promoting family–school partnerships (Frieman, 1994; Parker, 1994).

During divorce, social support for the family is typically lacking. Wallerstein and Blakeslee (1989) pointed out that unlike other family crises, during divorce, social support systems tend to fall away. The lack of emotional support that children and their families experience during the divorce can be improved by offering intervention through the schools (Richardson & Rosen, 1999). Thus, dissemination of information regarding effective school-based interventions for children of divorce and their families is essential. In Grych and Fincham's (1992) review, they noted that there is little empirical documentation validating the efficacy of school-based interventions for children of divorce. Richardson and Rosen (1999), however, identified four models, in particular, that present solid empirical evidence (e.g., Goldman & King, 1985; Pedro-Carroll, Alpert-Gillis, & Cowen,1992; Sanders & Riester,1996; Stolberg & Mahler,1989, 1994).

Goldman and King (1985) designed a school-based program for elementary school-age children and young adolescents that incorporates group work, teacher training, and parent involvement. The groups met for 50–75 minutes during a 6–12 week period dictated by the school schedule and calendar. During group time, children engaged in a variety of activities and discussed various topics, such as drawing good and bad changes, charades of various feelings, visualization, and coping skills. Parent involvement included meeting with group leaders, completing questionnaires, and a one-time meeting of all the parents of children in the group. Goldman and King (1985) found that children who were just beginning to experience divorce in the family showed more improvement than children whose parents had been divorced for more than 2 years, which emphasizes the need for early intervention in the schools. After completing the group, 95% of the children who participated in the intervention reported positive and enthusiastic reactions to the group, especially the peer support they experienced while in the group.

Pedro-Carroll, Alpert-Gillis, and Cowen (1992) developed the Children of Divorce Intervention Program (CODIP), which is a preventive education program that addresses the emotional and behavioral problems many children experience when parents are divorcing. CODIP rests on the prevention theory that timely interventions for people experiencing stressful life changes can offer important short- and long-term benefits (Pedro-Carroll, Sutton, & Wyman, 1999). Throughout the group sessions, there are a number of specific goals emphasized. Leaders strive to provide a supportive group environment that helps children identify and express their feelings. Understanding divorce-related concepts and clarifying divorce-related misconceptions are also fundamental goals of the group. Additionally, the group helps kids develop skills in social problem solving, effective communication, support seeking, and appropriate expression of their anger. Group time is also spent helping the kids to establish positive perceptions of themselves and their families (Pedro-Carroll, Alpert-Gillis, & Cowen, 1992). The CODIP was found to be effective in benefiting children's adjustment to the divorce: There was diminished anxiety, and the children held fewer negative attributions about themselves and their families (Pedro-Carroll & Alpert-Gillis, 1997; Pedro-Carroll, Alpert-Gillis, & Cowen, 1992; Pedro-Carroll, Sutton, & Wyman, 1999).

Another empirically supported program was designed by Sanders and Riester (1996) and involves a 10-week intervention that consists of 30 minutes of group sessions for the students once weekly. Parental involvement was not reported. The group sessions include a variety of discussions (e.g., what is divorce; why people get divorced; feelings experienced; coping with feelings, guilt, and divided loyalties; familial changes; custody and new living arrangements; and stepfamilies). They found that the intervention resulted in improved peer relations, seemed to have helped participants feel more socially accepted, and seemed to normalize their feelings about the divorce.

Stolberg and Mahler (1989, 1994) developed a 14-week school-based intervention for which they assigned participants to one of four groups: support; support and skill building; support, skill building, and transfer; or the control group that involved only parent training in responding to their child's concerns about and reactions to the divorce. Their model yielded significant adjustive gains for students who participated in the skill-building components, which helped them to label and express feelings. However, the support-alone condition yielded the most significant benefits for the children with significant problems at home and at school. At follow-up, this group also showed the greatest reductions in clinical symptomology.

Parent Education

Crase, Carlson, and Kontos (1981) concluded that when parents experience child-rearing problems, they often turn to school counselors for assistance. Some school counselors have initiated parent education or parent skills programs to reach effectively a group of parents rather than consulting one on one with each parent. In a survey of school counselors, Ritchie and Partin (1994) found that the majority of school counselors felt there was a substantial need for parent skills training in their community. There are a number of commercial programs that counselors can purchase, such as Active Parenting (Popkin, 1983), Parents Effectiveness Training (PET; Gordon, 1970), and Systematic Training for Effective Parenting (STEP; Dinkmeyer & McKay, 1976). Ritchie and Partin found that the STEP program had the most widespread use among school counselors. The STEP program is mainly based on Alderian theory and stresses the importance of parents using natural and logical consequences.

There is support for the effectiveness of parenting programs. In a meta-analysis of the PET program, Cedar and Levant (1990) found that it was moderately effective in terms of positively affecting children's self-esteem and parents' knowledge, attitudes, and behaviors. They also found that PET was more effective than alternative parent education programs; however, this finding is somewhat tenuous because of the methodological limitations of this study. The research concerning the effectiveness of the STEP program is not as substantial as compared with the PET program. Some researchers (Brooks, Spearn, Rice, & Crocco, 1988; Dinkmeyer, McKay, & Dinkmeyer, 1990) have concluded that STEP is effective, whereas others have concluded that other parenting programs are more effective than STEP (Ratzlaff, Friesen, Neufeld, & Paddock, 1989). Parent management training has been found to be effective with children with clinical problems, such as attention deficit-hyperactivity disorder (ADHD), oppositional and conduct disorders, and delinquency (Estrada & Pinsof, 1995). This program focuses on specific problem behaviors and uses modeling, role-playing, and home practice. In addition, there is support for programs designed to increase the communication and behavior management skills of low-income parents (James & Etheridge, 1983).

The research seems to reflect that teaching parenting skills to children's parents can be beneficial for children with behavioral problems and can also be effective in preventing future problems for many children. Given the preventative focus of school counselors, it seems that parent education programs should be a component of a comprehensive school counseling program, particularly at the elementary level. Sometimes parent education programs are offered in schools, yet very few parents participate. School counselors need to consider ways of providing these programs that will motivate parents to attend, such as starting the program the week after parent-teacher conferences. Furthermore, school counselors need to offer these programs at times and locations that support parent involvement.

Family Therapy

Sutton (1999) argued that it is important to work with families when children begin experiencing behavioral and emotional difficulties, before the behavioral difficulties become entrenched. Both qualitative reviews (Alexander & Barton, 1996; Gurman, Kniskern, & Pinsof, 1986) and meta-analyses (Hazelrigg, Cooper, & Bourdin, 1987; Shadish et al., 1993) have concluded that family therapy is an effective method of intervening with a wide range of client problems. What is particularly compelling about the family therapy literature is the research indicating that family counseling may be one of the most effective methods of treating many of the behavioral problems of adolescents and children. Hence, school counselors may want to strive to provide family counseling in schools because the research clearly indicates that these are the most effective interventions with certain behavioral problems.

A number of recent, highly publicized school shootings (e.g., Columbine High School) have resulted in increased public interest in school violence and prevention activities. Youth violence is a national issue, with 30% to 40% of males and 16% to 32% of females having committed a serious violent offense by age 17 (U.S. Surgeon General, 2001). Hundreds of youth violence prevention programs have been initiated in schools and communities throughout the country, but there has been little evaluation of the effectiveness of these programs. Mendel (2000) found that much of the money spent on youth violence prevention is spent on ineffective (and sometimes even harmful) programs and policies. School counselors, certainly, do not have the time or the resources to initiate programs that are ineffectual or that might even increase violence. Therefore, it seems important for school counselors to incorporate programs with substantial empirical support. Elliott (1998) conducted a rigorous examination of existing intervention programs for youth violence with the intention of identifying effective programs based on substantial empirical evidence. Of the 500 programs reviewed, only 10 programs met the rigorous standards used. The U.S. surgeon general and the Centers for Disease Control and Prevention have endorsed these 10 programs as effective programs in violence prevention. Of the 10 programs deemed effective, only 2 of those were counseling-related programs, and both of these were family-based counseling approaches (i.e., functional family therapy and multisystemic therapy). The other effective seven approaches were psychoeducational, residential, and community-based interventions, such as prenatal and infancy home visitations or foster care treatment.

The primary sources of scientific evidence for functional family therapy (FFT) and multisystemic therapy (MST) are well-designed research studies that are conducted in "real life" settings (Sexton & Alexander, in press). Not only do these two approaches appear to be effective with aggression-related and conduct disorder problems, but there also is evidence that these two programs are cost-effective. In a comprehensive analysis of the outcome and cost-effectiveness of various approaches to reducing delinquency, Aos and Barnoski (1998) found that functional family therapy and multisystemic therapy were among the most effective programs and had the highest cost savings when compared with other juvenile offender programs. The cost savings (taxpayer and crime victim costs) for MST and FFT ranged from $13,908 to $21,863 (per adolescent treated), respectively.

Family therapy also appears to be effective in the treatment of drug abuse for adolescents (Stanton & Shadish, 1997). In addition, Stanton and Shadish found that individuals were less likely to drop out of family treatment as compared with nonfamily drug treatment approaches. Another promising approach to family therapy, multidimensional family therapy, has been shown to be effective in adolescent substance abuse (Liddle & Dakof, 1995). In addition to decreasing drug use, this approach to family therapy resulted in students' grades improving. Functional family therapy and MST have also been found effective in reducing adolescent drug use and increasing school attendance (Sexton & Alexander, in press). The relationship between family therapy and the academic variables of grades and attendance is another reason for including family therapy in school counseling programs. It further appears that family therapy can be used with families from diverse ethnic backgrounds. Using culturally sensitive engagement strategies, Szapocznik, Kurtines, Santisteban, and Rio (1990) found that family therapy was more effective than individual therapy in influencing Latino adolescents' drug use.

Although there is considerable support for the efficacy of family therapy, Shadish et al. (1993) clearly demonstrated that not all approaches to family therapy are equally effective. Therefore, school counselors cannot approach family counseling with a generic approach but need detailed information about which approaches work best for which family situations. There is substantial empirical support for FFT and MST, and school counselors may want to investigate these two therapeutic models. Becoming competent in family therapy, however, cannot occur without substantial training and supervision. Although school counselors may have a course in family dynamics or family counseling, one course will not provide sufficient training to initiate family therapy. Although there is substantial empirical support for family therapy, school counselors without sufficient training should refrain from providing these services because it is unethical to practice outside of areas of competence.

Conclusion

The purpose of this chapter is to provide school counselors with information on which school counseling activities researchers have found to be effective. This research, however, is somewhat limited because there has been very little research on school counseling programs. Many school counselors are instituting school counseling programs that are designed to assist all students (Campbell & Dahir, 1997; Gysbers & Henderson, 2000), yet we know very little about the effectiveness of these programs. The need for programmatic research in school counseling is critical with the current trend toward empirically supported programs in education. School counselors need to become involved with research projects that examine whether school counseling programs facilitate student development and determine the critical factors of an effective school counseling program. The need for this type of research is crucial because school counseling programs could easily be eliminated if there are not more empirical investigations of the effects of these programs.

Although we need to know more about the critical factors in an effective school counseling program, there are some findings that indicate students from schools with more fully implemented school counseling perform better in school and view their educational environment more positively than students from schools with less of a programmatic focus. Research findings also indicate that effective school counseling programs have school counselors working with students, rather than performing clerical and paperwork duties. There is empirical support for providing both individual and group counseling to students. Career counseling and courses designed to facilitate career development have been found to be effective. Furthermore, skillful consultation with parents and teachers has been found to have a positive effect on a number of student outcomes.

There are other school counseling activities, however, for which the research is more equivocal, and school counselors should not conclude that these activities have sufficient empirical support. The research related to both guidance curriculum activities and peer mediation programs reflects mixed results, with some studies indicating these activities have a positive effect on students, and other studies reflecting that these activities are not helpful to students. It may be that certain guidance curriculum activities produce positive outcomes if the guidance curriculum is developmentally appropriate and provided by a skilled clinician. It is often difficult to ascertain the theoretical or research base school counselors use in selecting guidance curriculum activities; more sound approaches to designing guidance curriculum activities may result in better outcomes. In addition, peer mediation programs may be more successful if trained counselors coordinate them. Counseling and communication skills also seem to be important in drug intervention programs, for which the research findings reflect that more effective programs facilitate student involvement.

Given the substantial empirical support for working with families and not just the students within a school, school counselors should consider methods of incorporating more family interventions into their daily activities. There is particular support for conducting groups for children experiencing divorce or family transitions, parenting skills or parent education programs, and family therapy. Given the current concerns about school violence, it is important to note that two family therapy approaches have been endorsed by both the U.S. surgeon general and the Centers for Disease Control and Prevention as programs that meet the scientific standards for preventing youth violence. These two programs have strict protocols that must be followed, and training is required to provide these services. In our opinion, this may be an important time for school counselors to take an active role in preventing youth violence by seeking training in one of these two empirically supported family therapy approaches.

References

Alexander, J. F., & Barton, C. (1996). Family therapy research. In R. H. Mikesell, D. Lusterman, & S. H. McDaniel (Eds.), *Integrating family therapy: Handbook of family psychology* (pp. 199–216). Washington, DC: American Psychological Association.

Aos, S., & Barnoski, R. (1998). *Watching the bottom line: Cost-effective interventions for reducing crime in Washington.* Oympia, WA: Washington State Institute for Public Policy.

Baker, S. B., Swisher, J. D., Nadenickek, P. E., & Popowicz, C. L. (1984). Measured effects of primary prevention strategies. *Personnel and Guidance Journal, 62,* 459–464.

Baker, S. B., & Taylor, J. G. (1998). Effects of career education interventions: A meta-analysis. *Career Development Quarterly, 46,* 376–385.

Bauer, S. R., Sapp, M., & Johnson, D. (2000). Group counseling strategies for rural at-risk high school students. *High School Journal, 83,* 41–50.

Bisnaire, L. M. C., Firestone, P., & Rynard, D. (1990). Factors associated with academic achievement in children following parental separation. *American Journal of Orthopsychiatry, 60*(1), 67–76.

Borders, L. D., & Drury, S. M. (1992). Comprehensive school counseling programs: A review for policymakers and practitioners. *Journal of Counseling & Development, 70,* 487–498.

Brooks, L. D., Spearn, R. C., Rice, M., & Crocco, D. (1988). Systematic training for effective parenting. *Canada's Mental Health, 36*(4), 2–5.

Campbell, C. A., & Dahir, C. A. (1997). *The national standards for school counseling programs.* Alexandria, VA: American School Counselor Association.

Cantrell, R. G. (1986). Adjustment to divorce: Three components to assist children. *Elementary School Guidance and Counseling, 20,* 163–173.

Cedar, B., & Levant, R. F. (1990). A meta-analysis of the effects of parent effectiveness training. *American Journal of Family Therapy, 18,* 373–384.

Crase, S. J., Carlson, C., & Kontos, S. (1981). Parent education needs and sources as perceived by parents. *Home Economics Research, 9,* 221–231.

Dinkmeyer, D., & McKay, G. D. (1976). *Systematic training for effective parenting.* Circle Pines, MN: American Guidance Service.

Dinkmeyer, D., McKay, G. D., Dinkmeyer, D., Jr. (1990). Inaccuracy in STEP research reporting. *Canadian Journal of Counselling, 24,* 103–105.

Elliott, D. S. (1998). Editor's introduction. In D. S. Elliott (Ed.), *Blueprints for violence prevention* (pp. i–xi). Boulder, CO: Center for the Study and Prevention of Violence.

Estrada, A. U., & Pinsof, W. M. (1995). The effects of family therapies for selective behavioral disorders of childhood. *Journal of Marital and Family Therapy, 21,* 403–440.

Evensen, D. H., & Hmelo, C. E. (2000). *Problem-based learning: A research perspective on learning interactions.* Mahwah, NJ: Lawrence Erlbaum.

Frieman, B. B. (1994). Children of divorced parents: Action steps for the counselor to involve fathers. *Elementary School Guidance and Counseling, 28*(3), 197–205.

Gerler, E. R. (1985). Elementary school counseling research and the class-room learning environment. *Elementary School Guidance and Counseling, 20,* 39–40.

Goldman, R. K., & King, M. J. (1985). Counseling children of divorce. *School Psychology Review, 14*(3), 280–290.

Gordon, T. (1970). *Parent effectiveness training.* New York: Wyden.

Gresham, F. M., & Kendell, G. K. (1987). School consultation research: Methodological critique and future research direction. *School Psychology Review, 16,* 306–316.

Grych, J. H., & Fincham, F. D. (1992). Interventions for children of divorce: Toward greater integration of research and action. *Psychological Bulletin, 111,* 434–454.

Guidubaldi, J., Cleminshaw, H. D., Perry, J. D., & Mcloughlin, C. S. (1983). The impact of parental divorce on children: Report of the nationwide NASP study. *School Psychology Review, 12,* 300–323.

Gurman, A. S., Kniskern, D. P., & Pinsof, W. M. (1986). Research on the process and outcome of marital and family therapy. In S. L. Garfield & A. E. Bergin (Eds.), *Handbook of psychotherapy and behavior change* (3rd ed., pp. 565–624). New York: Wiley.

Gutkin, T. B., & Curtis, M. J. (1990). School-based consultation: Theory, techniques, and research. In T. B. Gutkin & C. R. Reynolds (Eds.), *The handbook of school psychology* (2nd ed., pp. 577–611). New York: Wiley.

Gysbers, N. C., & Henderson, P. (2000). *Developing and managing your school counseling program* (3rd ed.). Alexandria, VA: American Counseling Association.

Gysbers, N. C., Lapan, R. T., & Blair, M. (1999). Closing in on the statewide implementation of a comprehensive guidance program model. *Professional School Counseling, 2,* 357–366.

Hazelrigg, M., Cooper, H., & Borduin, C. (1987). Evaluating the effectiveness of family therapies: An integrative review and analysis. *Psychological Bulletin, 101,* 428–442.

James, R., & Etheridge, G. (1983). Does parent training change behavior in inner city children? *Elementary School Guidance and Counseling, 18,* 75–78.

Kiselica, M. S., Baker, S. B., Thomas, R. N., & Reddy, S. (1994). Effects of stress inoculation training on anxiety, stress, and academic performance among adolescents. *Journal of Counseling Psychology, 41,* 335–342.

Kraus, I. (1998). A fresh look at school counseling: A family-systems approach. *Professional School Counseling, 1,* 12–17.

Lambert, M. J. (1991). Introduction to psychotherapy research. In L. E. Beutler & M. Crago (Eds.), *Psychotherapy research: An international review of programmatic studies* (pp. 1–23). Washington, DC: American Psychological Association.

Lapan, R. T., Gysbers, N. C., & Sun, Y. (1997). The impact of more fully implemented guidance programs on the school experiences of high school students: A statewide evaluation study. *Journal of Counseling & Development, 75,* 292–302.

Lewis, M. W., & Lewis, A. C. (1996). Peer helping programs: Helper role, supervisor training, and suicidal behavior. *Journal of Counseling & Development, 74,* 307–313.

Lewis, M. W., & Lewis, A. C. (1999, October). *The efficacy of peer helping programs.* Paper presented at the Association for Counselor Education and Supervision, New Orleans, LA.

Lewis, W. (1996). A proposal for initiating family counseling interventions by school counselors. *The School Counselor, 44,* 93–99.

Liddle, H. A., & Dakof, G. A. (1995). Efficacy of family therapy for drug abuse: Promising but not definitive. *Journal of Marital and Family Therapy, 21,* 511–543.

Mendel, R. A. (2000). *Less hype, more help: Reducing juvenile crime, what works—and what doesn't.* Washington, DC: American Youth Policy Forum.

Myers, R. A. (1986). Research on educational and vocational counseling. In A. E. Bergin & S. L. Garfield (Eds.), *Handbook of psychotherapy and behavior change: An empirical analysis* (3rd ed., pp. 715–738). New York: Wiley.

National Reading Panel. (2000). *Report of the Reading Panel: Teaching children to read: An evidence-based assessment of the scientific research literature on reading and its implications for reading instruction.* Washington, DC: National Institute of Child Health and Development.

Oliver, L. W., & Spokane, A. R. (1988). Career-intervention outcome: What contributes to client gain? *Journal of Counseling Psychology, 35,* 447–462

Otwell, P. S., & Mullis, F. (1997). Counselor-led staff development: An efficient approach to teacher consultation. *Professional School Counseling, 1,* 25–30.

Parker, R. J. (1994). Helping children cope with divorce: A workshop for parents. *Elementary School Guidance and Counseling, 29*(2), 137–148.

Pedro-Carroll, J. L., & Alpert-Gillis, L. J. (1997). Prevention interventions for children of divorce: A developmental model for 5-and 6-year-old children. *Journal of Primary Prevention, 18,* 5–23.

Pedro-Carroll, J. L., Alpert-Gillis, L. J., & Cowen, E. L. (1992). An evaluation of the efficacy of a preventive intervention for 4th–6th grade urban children of divorce. *Journal of Primary Prevention, 13*(2), 115–120.

Pedro-Carroll, J. L., Sutton, S. E., & Wyman, P. A. (1999). A 2-year follow-up evaluation of a preventive intervention for young children of divorce. *School Psychology Review, 28*(3), 467–476.

Perry, N. S. (1993). School counseling. In G. R. Walz & J. C. Bleuer (Eds.), *Counselor efficacy: Assessing and using counseling outcome research* (pp. 37–49). Ann Arbor, MI: ERIC.

Popkin, M. (1983). *Active parenting.* Atlanta, GA: Active Parenting.

Prout, S. M., & Prout, H. T. (1998). A meta-analysis of school-based studies of counseling and psychotherapy: An update. *Journal of School Psychology, 36*, 121–136.

Ratzlaff, H. C., Friesen, J. D., Neufeld, G., & Paddock, G. M. (1989). Impact of the Creative Parenting program. *Canadian Journal of Counselling, 23*, 163–173.

Richardson, C. D., & Rosen, L. A. (1999). School-based interventions for children of divorce. *Professional School Counseling, 3*(1), 21–26.

Ritchie, M. A., & Partin, R. L. (1994). Parent education and consultation activities of school counselors. *The School Counselor, 41*, 165–170.

Sanders, D. R., & Riester, A. E. (1996). School-based counseling groups for children of divorce: Effects on the self-concepts of 5th grade children. *Journal of Child and Adolescent Group Therapy, 6*(1), 147–156.

Schmidt, J., Lanier, S., & Cope, L. (1999). *Elementary School Guidance and Counseling:* The last 20 years. *Professional School Counseling, 2*, 250–257.

Schmidt, J. J. (1995). Assessing school counseling programs through external reviews. *The School Counselor, 43*, 114–115.

Sexton, T. L. (1996). The relevance of counseling outcome research: Current trends and practical implications. *Journal of Counseling & Development, 74*, 590–600.

Sexton, T. L., & Alexander, J. F. (in press). Family-based empirically supported interventions. *The Counseling Psychologist.*

Shadish, W., Montgomery, L., Wilson, P., Wilson, M., Bright, I., & Okwumabua, T. (1993). Effects of family and marital psychotherapies: A meta-analysis. *Journal of Consulting and Clinical Psychology, 61*, 992–1002.

Shepard, K. K. (1994). Stemming conflict through peer mediation. *School Administrator, 51*, 14–17.

Stanton, M. D., & Shadish, W. R. (1997). Outcome, attrition, and family-couples treatment for drug abuse: A meta-analysis and review of the controlled, comparative studies. *Psychological Bulletin, 122*, 170–191.

Stolberg, A. L., & Mahler, J. (1989). Protecting children from the consequences of divorce: An empirically derived approach. *Prevention in Human Services, 7*, 161–176.

Stolberg, A. L., & Mahler, J. (1994). Enhancing treatment gains in a school-based intervention for children of divorce through skills training, parental involvement, and transfer procedures. *Journal of Consulting and Clinical Psychology, 62*, 147–156.

Sutton, C. (1999). *Helping families with troubled children: A prevention approach.* Chichester, UK: John Wiley.

Swanson, J. L. (1995). The process and outcome of career counseling. In W. B. Walsh & S. H. Osipow (Eds.), *The handbook of vocational psychology* (pp. 217–259). Mahwah, NJ: Lawrence Erlbaum.

Szapocznik, J., Kurtines, W., Santisteban, D. A., & Rio, A. T. (1990). Interplay of advances between theory, research, and application in treatment interventions aimed at behavior problem children and adolescents. *Journal of Consulting and Clinical Psychology, 58*, 696–703.

Tobler, N. (1994). Meta-analytical issues for prevention intervention research. In L. Seitz & L. Collins (Eds.), *Advances in data analysis for prevention intervention research* (NIDA Research Monograph 142, NIH Publication No. 94-3599, pp. 342–402). Washington, DC: U.S. Government Printing Office.

Tobler, N. S., & Stratton, H. H. (1997). Effectiveness of school-based drug prevention programs: A meta-analysis of the research. *Journal of Primary Prevention, 18*, 71–128.

U.S. Surgeon General. (2001). *Youth violence: A report of the Surgeon General.* Retrieved from http://www.surgeongeneral.gov/library/youthviolence/

Wallerstein, J. S., & Blakeslee, S. (1989). *Second chances.* New York: Tiknor & Fields.

Wampold, B. E., Lichtenberg, J. W., & Waehler, C. A. (in press). Principles of empirically supported interventions in counseling psychology. *The Counseling Psychologist.*

Whiston, S. C., & Sexton, T. L. (1998). A review of school counseling outcome research: Implications for practice. *Journal of Counseling and Development, 76*, 412–426.

Whiston, S. C., Sexton, T. L., & Lasoff, D. L. (1998). Career intervention outcome: A replication and extension. *Journal of Counseling Psychology, 45*, 150–165.

Wiggins, J. D., & Moody, A. H. (1987). Student evaluations of counseling programs: An added dimension. *The School Counselor, 34*(5), 353–361.

Zins, J. E. (1993). Enhancing consultee problem-solving skills in consultative interactions. *Journal of Counseling & Development, 72*, 185–190.

■ ■ ■